THE LOSER
(*LE DINDON*)

Georges Feydeau
Translated by
Laurence Senelick

BROADWAY PLAY PUBLISHING INC
New York
www.broadwayplaypublishing.com
info@broadwayplaypublishing.com

THE LOSER
© Copyright 2018 Laurence Senelick

Cover art by Leonetto Cappiello

First edition: May 2018
I S B N: 978-0-88145-776-6

Book design: Marie Donovan
Page make-up: Adobe InDesign
Typeface: Palatino

LE DINDON was first performed at the Théâtre du Palais-Royal 8 February 1896.

CHARACTERS

CRISPIN VATELIN, *a lawyer*
LUCIENNE, *his wife*
RÉDILLON, *a friend*
PONTAGNAC, *"the loser"*
CLOTILDE, *his wife*
SOLDIGNAC, *a Viennese from Marseille*
LIESL, *his wife*
PINCHARD, *an army doctor*
MME PINCHARD, *his wife*
ARMANDINE, *a lady of easy virtue*
GÉRÔME, RÉDILLON'S *valet*
JEAN, *the* VATELINS' *butler*
VICTOR, *a bellhop*
The MANAGER *of the hotel*
CLARA, *a chambermaid*
1ST POLICE INSPECTOR
2ND POLICE INSPECTOR
POLICEMEN; HOTEL GUESTS *and* TOURISTS *of both sexes*

ACT ONE

(The VATELINS's flat in Paris. An elegant drawing-room. A door at back. Two doors right, two left. Furniture includes several chairs and a desk.)

(As the curtain rises, the stage remains empty for a moment. Suddenly we hear noises at the back, and LUCIENNE *in street clothes, her hat somewhat askew, erupts on stage as if panic-stricken. She closes the door behind her, but not fast enough to keep a cane from being slipped in between the door and the door-frame.)*

LUCIENNE: Oh, for heaven's sake! Leave me alone, Monsieur! …Leave me alone!…

*(*PONTAGNAC, *trying to push the door open every time* LUCIENNE *pushes it shut:)*

PONTAGNAC: Madame! …Madame! …I beg of you!…

LUCIENNE: Absolutely not, Monsieur! …How can you behave like this! *(Shouting while struggling against the door.)* Jean, Jean! Augustine! …Oh, for heaven's sake, there's nobody here!…

PONTAGNAC: Madame, Madame!

LUCIENNE: No! No!

PONTAGNAC: *(Who has managed to get in)* I beg of you, Madame, listen to me.

LUCIENNE: This is outrageous! …I forbid you, Monsieur! …Get out!

PONTAGNAC: Don't be alarmed, Madame. I mean you
no harm! Even though my intentions are dishonorable,
I swear they aren't hostile…quite the reverse. *(He goes
to her.)*

LUCIENNE: *(Recoiling)* Never! Monsieur, you are out of
your mind!

PONTAGNAC: *(Pursuing her)* Absolutely right, Madame!
Driven out of my mind by you! I know my behavior
is outrageous, abnormal, but what do I care! …One
thing I'm sure of: I love you and will stop at nothing to
possess you.

LUCIENNE: *(Stopping short)* Monsieur, I refuse to listen
to any more of this! …Get out!…

PONTAGNAC: Ah! Anything, Madame, anything but
that! I tell you I love you! *(Fresh pursuit.)* The moment I
laid eyes on you I was smitten! I've been dogging your
steps for a week now! You must have noticed.

LUCIENNE: *(Stopping before the desk)* Not at all,
Monsieur.

PONTAGNAC: Yes, Madame, you *did* notice! A woman
always notices when a man is following her.

LUCIENNE: What conceit!

PONTAGNAC: It's not conceit, it's close observation.

LUCIENNE: But I don't know you, Monsieur.

PONTAGNAC: Nor do I know *you*, Madame, and I'm so
sorry about it that I'd like to end that state of affairs…
Ah! Madame…

LUCIENNE: Monsieur!

PONTAGNAC: Ah! Marguerite!

LUCIENNE: *(Forgetting)* My name's Lucienne!

PONTAGNAC: Thanks! Ah! Lucienne!

LUCIENNE: Monsieur, I forbid you! …Who gave you permission?…

PONTAGNAC: Didn't you just tell me your name?

LUCIENNE: What do you take me for, Monsieur? I'm a respectable woman!

PONTAGNAC: All the better! I adore respectable women!

LUCIENNE: Take care, Monsieur! I should like to avoid a scandal, but if you refuse to leave, I shall have to call my husband.

PONTAGNAC: What! You have a husband?

LUCIENNE: Certainly, Monsieur!

PONTAGNAC: Fine! Let's leave that imbecile out of this.

LUCIENNE: Imbecile! My husband!

PONTAGNAC: The husbands of women like you are always imbeciles.

LUCIENNE: (Crossing upstage) Very well! You'll see how the imbecile will deal with you! Will you leave?…

PONTAGNAC: Not likely.

LUCIENNE: (Calling right) All right! …Crispin!…

PONTAGNAC: What a stupid name!…

LUCIENNE: Crispin!…

(VATELIN enters.)

VATELIN: Did you call me, sweetheart?

PONTAGNAC: (Aside) Vatelin! Hell!

VATELIN: (Recognizing PONTAGNAC) Ah! Why, it's Pontagnac! My dear friend!

LUCIENNE: Eh!

PONTAGNAC: Good old Vatelin!

VATELIN: How are things?

PONTAGNAC: Fine, fine!

LUCIENNE: *(Aside)* They know one another. *(She comes down left, takes off her hat and puts it on the sofa.)*

PONTAGNAC: Well, what a surprise!

VATELIN: What d'you mean, "what a surprise"? You're in my house, you must have expected to see me.

PONTAGNAC: Huh? ...No... I mean, "What a surprise for you," eh?

VATELIN: Ah! Yes indeed!

LUCIENNE: This is too much! *(To* VATELIN*)* Do you know this gentleman?

VATELIN: Do I know him!

PONTAGNAC: *(Panicked)* Yes... yes, he kno... *(Losing his head, taking a coin from his pocket and putting it into* LUCIENNE's *hand.)* Here, take this! Not another word! Not a word!

LUCIENNE: *(Startled)* Huh! He gave me a gold-piece!

VATELIN: *(Who has missed this byplay)* Well, what's the matter with you?

PONTAGNAC: Me? Nothing! What could possibly be the matter?

*(*VATELIN *crosses a bit upstage.)*

LUCIENNE: *(In an undertone)* Monsieur, take this back! What am I supposed to do with this money?

PONTAGNAC: Oh! Excuse me, Madame! *(Aside)* I don't know what I'm doing! I'm losing my head!

VATELIN: Ah, good old Pontagnac! You really have no idea how touched I am by this! When I'd given up all hope of ever seeing you in my home, when you'd promised me so often...

LUCIENNE: Ah, you mean you can't thank the gentleman enough.

(PONTAGNAC *gets confused, bowing and greeting which ill conceal his nervousness.*)

VATELIN: Precisely! I can't tell you how glad I am you came, and especially the way you did it!

LUCIENNE: Yes, especially the way you did it! (*She heads for the fireplace.*)

PONTAGNAC: Really, dear friend, Madame! (*Aside*) She won't give me a break!

VATELIN: But I don't believe you've met my wife... (*Introducing*) My dear Lucienne, one of my best friends, Monsieur de Pontagnac... My wife.

PONTAGNAC: Madame!

VATELIN: Of course, I don't know whether it was very wise to introduce you to Pontagnac.

LUCIENNE: Why not?

VATELIN: Ah, he's such a playboy. Such a sinner in the eyes of the Almighty! Haven't you heard about him? He can't look at a woman without trying to seduce her! He wants to have them all!

LUCIENNE: (*Mocking*) All! Ah, that's not very flattering to any individual woman.

PONTAGNAC: Oh, Madame, he's exaggerating! (*Aside*) What an idiot, to tell her that!

LUCIENNE: (*In front of the fireplace*) How disappointing for the poor woman who thinks she's being singled out, and realizes at last that she's only being added up.

PONTAGNAC: Madame, I repeat, it's a slander.

LUCIENNE: I confess that if I had to be one of them "all", I wouldn't boast about it... Do sit down! (*She sits in an armchair beside the fireplace.*)

PONTAGNAC: *(Sitting on the sofa; aside)* Oh, fine! Now she's teasing me!

VATELIN: *(Sitting near them)* Say, I think she's needling you!

PONTAGNAC: So do I!

LUCIENNE: But, gentlemen, you must have a very low opinion of us, to see the way some of you treat us! We don't mind the courting: you have to be courteous to court! At least it shows a modicum of respect! But those men who expect to take us by storm, by following us in the street—really!

PONTAGNAC: *(Aside)* Uh-oh! Here it comes!

VATELIN: But what kind of men follow women in the street? Dirty old men, pimps and mental defectives…

LUCIENNE: *(Very politely to PONTAGNAC)* Take your pick!…

PONTAGNAC: *(Embarrassed)* But, Madame, I don't know why you ask me…

VATELIN: Oh, my wife was speaking in the abstract.

LUCIENNE: Of course!

PONTAGNAC: Fine! *(Aside)* Amazing what unpleasant subjects some people choose to talk about!

LUCIENNE: Well, I don't know what you think, but it seems to me that if I were a man, I wouldn't favor that means of attack. Because there two possibilities: either the woman gives me the brush-off and I'm no better off than before, a waste of time! Or she would welcome me with open arms, which would certainly eliminate any desire for *that* woman.

PONTAGNAC: *(Embarrassed)* Yes, of course!… *(Aside)* How long are we going to keep up this witty banter?

LUCIENNE: Yes, but all men don't seem to share that opinion, judging by the one who insists on following me.

PONTAGNAC: *(Aside)* She's going too far!

VATELIN: *(Rising and crossing to his wife)* There's a man been following you?

LUCIENNE: All the time!

PONTAGNAC: *(Rising and coming downstage)* Good grief! Suppose we change the subject. This conversation is becoming…

VATELIN: Certainly not! This is intriguing! Can you imagine some man has the nerve to follow my wife!

PONTAGNAC: Oh, but ever so discreetly!

VATELIN: How do *you* know? Any man who follows a woman is always indiscreet. But why didn't you tell me this sooner?

LUCIENNE: Bah! What for? I considered him a harmless sort of philanderer…

PONTAGNAC: *(Aside)* Thanks!

VATELIN: But you might at least find a way to get rid of him. It must be tiresome to have a creature like that dogging your footsteps!

LUCIENNE: Oh! ever so tiresome!

VATELIN: And, besides, I find it humiliating. You should have, I don't know…taken a cab…gone into a shop.

LUCIENNE: I did. I went into a pastry shop, and he came in after me.

VATELIN: Well, when a man's following you, you don't go into a pastry shop, you go into a jeweller's. Why didn't you go into a jewelry shop?

LUCIENNE: I tried. He waited for me outside.

PONTAGNAC: *(Aside)* Oh Lord!

VATELIN: That so? ...Tenacious *and* experienced! *(To PONTAGNAC)* Really, my dear fellow, it's inconceivable how many boors there are in Paris!

PONTAGNAC: Oh, boor is rather, uh! ...suppose we change the subject...

VATELIN: To think that a husband can't let his wife step outdoors without exposing her to the rudeness of some slimy lecher...

(LUCIENNE rises and goes to sit on the hassock.)

PONTAGNAC: *(Furious)* Vatelin!

VATELIN: What?

PONTAGNAC: *(Restraining himself)* You're going too far!

VATELIN: Not at all! Can't go too far! ...Ah, I'd like to get my hands on that two-bit Casanova!

LUCIENNE: *(On the hassock)* Well, that's easy enough, isn't it, Monsieur de Pontagnac?

PONTAGNAC: For Heaven's sake... Uh! What time is it?

VATELIN: What? Does he know the man?

LUCIENNE: Better than anyone... Tell us his name, Monsieur de Pontagnac?

PONTAGNAC: *(On pins and needles)* No, Madame! How can I...

LUCIENNE: Yes, you can, you can! ...His name is... Pon... ta... come on... Pontawhat?

PONTAGNAC: Pontawhat! That's possible!

LUCIENNE: Pontagnac!

PONTAGNAC: *(Hollow laugh)* My goodness, yes... it was me! Heh heh! It was me!

VATELIN: *(Bursts out laughing)* Ha, ha, ha! what a card!

(LUCIENNE *rises and goes to the fireplace.*)

PONTAGNAC: Oh, it was because I knew who she was…
I knew it was Madame Vatelin, so I thought: Well, I'll
mystify her, I'll pretend to follow her…

LUCIENNE: *(Aside)* "Pretend" is clever! *(She stands before
the fireplace.)*

PONTAGNAC: And she'll be nicely surprised when we
meet face to face at her husband's.

VATELIN: Poppycock! You're making this up! Well,
that'll teach you to follow women! You hit on a friend's
wife, and made fine headway! …Learn your lesson!

PONTAGNAC: Well, I admit it! No hard feelings, I hope?

VATELIN: Me? Come on! …I know you're a friend…
and so! …Anyway, what annoys me about this sort of
thing—because, after all, I trust my wife—is looking
like a fool. A man follows my wife, he may know who
she is. He meets me, he thinks, "Well, well, here's the
husband of the lady I was following." I end up looking
like a jerk. But *you*, you see, know that I know. I know
that you know that I know. We know that we know
that we know! So I don't mind, I don't end up looking
like a jerk!

PONTAGNAC: That's obvious!

VATELIN: If anyone's annoyed, it's you!

PONTAGNAC: Me?

VATELIN: Well, it's always embarrassing to put your
foot in it.

PONTAGNAC: With a happy ending, since it enabled me
to see you again.

VATELIN: Oh, the pleasure's all mine, I assure you!

PONTAGNAC: You're too kind!

VATELIN: Not at all!

LUCIENNE: *(Aside)* Aren't they touching? *(Aloud)* I'm really delighted to see the two of us such close friends. *(She sits on the sofa.)*

VATELIN: Now all you have to do is apologize to my wife.

PONTAGNAC: *(To* LUCIENNE*)* Ah, Madame, you must think me very wicked. *(He crosses to the fireplace.)*

LUCIENNE: You bachelors are all like.

VATELIN: Bachelor, him! Why, he's married!

PONTAGNAC: *(Embarrassed)* Yes… a little!…

LUCIENNE: Why, that's awful!

PONTAGNAC: You think so?

LUCIENNE: Why, that's horrible! …How can it be that…?

PONTAGNAC: Well, you know how these things happen! …One fine day, you meet at the Registry Office… you don't know how, force of circumstance… The city clerk asks you questions… you answer "yes," just because there are people there, but when everyone's gone, you realize you're married. For life.

LUCIENNE: Monsieur, you are unforgiveable!

PONTAGNAC: *(Sitting in the armchair)* For being married?

LUCIENNE: No, for being married and behaving in this way. Really, what does Madame Pontagnac have to say about your behavior?

PONTAGNAC: You don't suppose I'm in the habit of keeping her informed.

LUCIENNE: Nice dealings! If you believe your goings-on are decent.

PONTAGNAC: Oh! oh!

LUCIENNE: Honestly! You would consider it indecent to fritter away the slightest portion of your wife's money, but when it concerns her private property, what belongs to her, a bulwark of the social order, marital fidelity, ah! you throw it away. "Who wants to break off a piece, step right up, who'll be the first? Roll up, roll up! There'll always be plenty left!" So you squander it! You squander it! What do you care? It's your wife who suffers! And you consider that decent?

PONTAGNAC: For pity's sake! If I'm assumed to have enough to meet the household expenses, why not spend the loose change…

LUCIENNE: Indeed!

PONTAGNAC: After all, when Rothschild…

LUCIENNE: First off, you're no Rothschild… or if you ever were, you're starting to lose some of your millions.

PONTAGNAC: How do *you* know?

VATELIN: *(Standing beside* LUCIENNE*)* She's hard on you.

LUCIENNE: And even if you still have it all! The funds don't belong to you anymore! You made them over to your wife. You haven't the right to dispose of property that's been transferred.

PONTAGNAC: Excuse me, but the capital hasn't been touched! Here it is! Intact! You must allow me to invest some of the interest. Note that, by the marriage contract, I administer the property. Well then! So long as I keep most of it in government bonds, you can't condemn me for making a few investments in foreign speculations.

LUCIENNE: If you're married, your only investments should be as the father of a family!

PONTAGNAC: You're talking like a trust lawyer.

LUCIENNE: Yes, well, I'd like to hear what you'd have to say if your wife did the same thing.

PONTAGNAC: There's no comparison.

LUCIENNE: *(Rising and coming downstage)* Oh, of course not, naturally there's no comparison! It's never the same thing to you men! You deserve to have your wife gamble away some of the common funds at roulette or twenty-one or sixty-nine.

VATELIN: *(Coming downstage)* Take care, Lucienne! If you keep preaching morality, Pontagnac will take a dislike to you.

LUCIENNE: I'm not preaching just for his benefit! It's for you, in case you ever get it into your head to follow Monsieur Pontagnac's example.

VATELIN: Me? Oh!

LUCIENNE: It'll be a big mistake to follow in his footsteps, because you know that I won't hesitate.

VATELIN: *(Shaking his head)* Twenty-one or sixty-nine!

LUCIENNE: I won't need that many! I'll take one lover and that'll be enough!

PONTAGNAC: *(With barely concealed glee)* Really!

VATELIN: See here, you sound pleased.

PONTAGNAC: Me? Not at all! "Really" means "Incredible"!

LUCIENNE: I've never met Madame Pontagnac, but I feel sorry for her.

PONTAGNAC: You're telling me, Madame? I never cheat on her without feeling sorry for her.

LUCIENNE: You must feel sorry for her pretty often!

VATELIN: Anyway, now that you know the way to our house, I hope you'll bring Madame Pontagnac here! My wife and I would be delighted to make her acquaintance.

PONTAGNAC: *(Aside)* My wife! Not likely! *(Aloud)* Dear me, by all means, I'd be happy to, so would she. Unfortunately, it's out of the question.

LUCIENNE: How so?

PONTAGNAC: On account of her rheumatism. She's bedridden with rheumatism…

VATELIN: Is that so!

PONTAGNAC: She never goes out, or, if she does, it's in a little cart. It's pulled by a flunkey…

VATELIN: Pulled by a donkey…

PONTAGNAC: No, a flunkey.

VATELIN: Worse yet! Ah, but I didn't know.

LUCIENNE: How painful it must be!

PONTAGNAC: You're telling me!

VATELIN: That's a real shame! But we'll go and pay her a visit, if you'll permit!

PONTAGNAC: What! Why of course!

VATELIN: Where does she live?

PONTAGNAC: On the Riviera.

VATELIN: Hell! That's a bit of a distance.

PONTAGNAC: There's an express train! …I can't help it, the doctor recommended the South of France for her health.

VATELIN: We'll have to leave her there.

LUCIENNE: But we *are* sorry.

JEAN: *(Enters at the back)* Monsieur, there's an art dealer who's brought a landscape for Monsieur.

VATELIN: Ah! my Corot! I bought a Corot yesterday!

PONTAGNAC: That so?

VATELIN: Six hundred francs!

PONTAGNAC: Not so expensive! Is it signed?

(LUCIENNE *goes to sit right of the desk.*)

VATELIN: It is signed. It's signed Poitevin, but the dealer guaranteed that the signature is a forgery.

PONTAGNAC: You don't say so?

VATELIN: I'll have Poitevin removed and only the Corot will be left... (*To* JEAN) Fine, I'm coming, show him into my study...

(JEAN *exits.*)

VATELIN: Excuse me a moment! I'll see the dealer and then I'll be with you! Wait, I'll show you my paintings, you're a man of taste! You can give me your opinion! (*He exits up right.*)

PONTAGNAC: All right!

LUCIENNE: Sit down.

PONTAGNAC: I don't frighten you anymore.

LUCIENNE: As you see.

PONTAGNAC: (*Sitting*) I must have seemed ridiculous.

LUCIENNE: (*Smiling*) You think so?

PONTAGNAC: You're teasing me!

LUCIENNE: Well...tell me, what did you hope to gain by following me so implacably?

PONTAGNAC: Good Lord! What any man hopes from the unknown woman he follows.

LUCIENNE: You're honest.

PONTAGNAC: Well, if I told you I was following you to ask your opinion of Voltaire, you probably wouldn't have believed me.

LUCIENNE: You do amuse me. And does this little maneuver succeed very often? …Are there really women who…?

PONTAGNAC: *Are* there? …Thirty-three and one third percent.

LUCIENNE: *(Nodding)* Aha! Well, you were out of luck today. You ran into one of the sixty-six and two thirds percent. *(She rises.)*

PONTAGNAC: *(Puts down his hat and cane and rises)* Oh, let's drop the subject, Madame. I can't help it, it's too much for me. I have women on the brain.

LUCIENNE: But the City Clerk very properly bestowed one on you.

PONTAGNAC: My wife, yes. Oh, she's charming, of course. But she's been charming to me for so long! She's a novel whose pages I have riffled so often.

LUCIENNE: Not to mention how hard it must have been to turn those pages.

PONTAGNAC: How do you mean?

LUCIENNE: Well, what with her rheumatism.

PONTAGNAC: Her…? Since when?

LUCIENNE: You were the one who told us…

PONTAGNAC: *(Quickly)* Ah, my wife, yes, yes…on the Riviera… Exactly! …Well, what about it?

LUCIENNE: Uh…

PONTAGNAC: And to tell me I have no excuse! Come, come! So, when Fate puts an exquisite, divine female in my path!…

LUCIENNE: *(Crossing left)* That will do, Monsieur! That's enough on that subject! I thought you made a suitable apology.

PONTAGNAC: Come on, confess it frankly, you're in love with someone else.

LUCIENNE: Really, Monsieur, your impertinence is becoming epic! Can't you accept the fact that a woman might be a faithful spouse? If she resists you, she has to be in love with someone else! There's no other motive! What sort of women do you frequent?

PONTAGNAC: Listen, will you promise never to confide to anyone what I'm about to tell you?

LUCIENNE: (*Sitting in the armchair*) Not even to my husband.

PONTAGNAC: (*Sitting on the hassock*) That's all I ask. Well! I can hardly believe you love him.

LUCIENNE: What an idea! Move away.

(PONTAGNAC *brings the hassock even closer.*)

LUCIENNE: No, move *away.*

PONTAGNAC: (*Moving the hassock away*) Oh, excuse me! …Of course he's an excellent fellow! I'm very fond of him.

LUCIENNE: I saw that right away.

PONTAGNAC: But, between you and me, he's not a man capable of inspiring passion.

LUCIENNE: (*Harshly*) He's my husband!

PONTAGNAC: (*Rising*) There, you see, you agree with me.

LUCIENNE: Not in the least!

PONTAGNAC: Yes you do! You do! If you did love him, really love him—I'm not talking about affection— would you need a motive for your love? A loving wife says "I love because I love". She doesn't say "I love because he's my husband". Love isn't a result, it's a principle! Its only existence, its only value is in its essence, but you serve it up to us as an extract.

LUCIENNE: You sound like a perfumer.

PONTAGNAC: What does his being a husband prove! Anyone can be a husband! So long as the family agrees to it… and he gets an exemption from the draft board! He needs only enough talent to get a job as a lawyer or a civil servant. *(Sitting on the hassock)* Whereas a lover is above all that. He must have passion! He is the poet of love. The husband is merely its pen-pusher

LUCIENNE: And so, no doubt, you come as a poet of love…

PONTAGNAC: Yes indeed!

LUCIENNE: No, my dear sir, no. I may perhaps strike you as absurd, but I am lucky enough to have a husband who constitutes both your categories: the pen-pusher and what you call the poet of love.

PONTAGNAC: Most unusual!

LUCIENNE: But it's all I require, and just because he doesn't wear his poetic qualities on his sleeve…

PONTAGNAC: Don't tell me he wears them…

LUCIENNE: *(Rising)* On his sleeve! That would be something else again. If I *were* to change my mind, I would go the whole hog.

PONTAGNAC: *(Rising)* Ah, how good of you!

LUCIENNE: Don't mention it! All or nothing…as I was saying the other day to…

PONTAGNAC: *(Seeing that she has stopped)* To whom?

LUCIENNE: To a niece of mine who kept insisting on knowing whether I would make up my mind some day.

PONTAGNAC: *(Disbelieving)* A niece?

(JEAN *enters at back.*)

JEAN: *(Announcing and withdrawing)* Monsieur Rédillon.

(RÉDILLON *enters at back.*)

LUCIENNE: Come in, dear friend, and help me convince this gentleman. *(Introducing)* Monsieur Ernest Rédillon, Monsieur de Pontagnac, a friend of my husband…and vice-versa.

(PONTAGNAC *and* RÉDILLON *bow to one another.*)

LUCIENNE: You know what I'm like, Rédillon. Tell this gentleman that I am a model wife and would never cheat on Monsieur Vatelin, unless he set the example.

RÉDILLON: Huh? What? Why this question?

LUCIENNE: Please! The gentleman wanted to know.

RÉDILLON: *(Put out)* The gentleman? Ah! This gentleman… Charming conversation, I must say. Given its topic, I wonder if I do not perchance intrude.

LUCIENNE: On the contrary, I appeal for your assistance.

PONTAGNAC: We were joking.

RÉDILLON: Is that so? Monsieur is unquestionably an old…old friend, an intimate, although I have never seen him in this house before.

LUCIENNE: Monsieur? I've known him for twenty minutes.

RÉDILLON: Better and better! I'm sorry, dear lady, that I cannot answer the question you ask, because I have too much respect for women to broach certain topics of conversation which I would consider inappropriate… on my lips. I declare myself incompetent. *(He goes up right.)*

PONTAGNAC: *(Aside)* Is this young man trying to show me up?

RÉDILLON: Isn't Vatelin in?

LUCIENNE: Yes, in the other room, in private session with a Corot! I'll see if he got lost in the landscape and bring him here. You've been introduced, you know one another! I leave you alone together.

(PONTAGNAC *and* RÉDILLON *bow.* LUCIENNE *exits right. A moment of silence. The two men take the measure of one another on the sly.*)

PONTAGNAC: (*After a pause; aside*) That man must be her niece!

(*Dumb show. Both men go up to the back and look at the paintings. Each gradually comes downstage, one on the right, one on the left. Every so often they steal a glance at one another on the sly, but affecting indifference whenever their glances meet.* RÉDILLON *reaches the sofa, drops on to it and begins to whistle.*)

PONTAGNAC: (*Seated beside the desk*) Beg pardon?

RÉDILLON: Monsieur?

PONTAGNAC: I thought you were talking to me.

RÉDILLON: Not at all!

PONTAGNAC: I beg your pardon!

RÉDILLON: No harm done… (*He goes on whistling.*) Ssi, ssi, ssi, ssi, ssi, ssi, ssi, ssi, ssi!

PONTAGNAC: (*After a pause, annoyed, begins to hum a different tune*) Hu, hu, hu, hu, hu, hu, hu.

(RÉDILLON *has drawn a newspaper from his pocket and, seated on the sofa, turns his back to* PONTAGNAC *and starts to read.* PONTAGNAC, *who has spotted a magazine on the desk, starts to leaf through it casually.* LUCIENNE *re-enters.*)

LUCIENNE: I hope I haven't interrupted your conversation.

(RÉDILLON *closes his newspaper,* PONTAGNAC *his magazine.*)

LUCIENNE: My husband is asking for you, Monsieur Pontagnac, he insists on showing you his Corot.

PONTAGNAC: Ah, he insists!…

LUCIENNE: It's through there, keep to the right.

PONTAGNAC: *(Starting out, unenthusiastically)* Through here?

LUCIENNE: Yes, that's right, go on.

PONTAGNAC: *(Picking up his hat and cane from the desk)* Yes, yes… *(After a pause)* Would this gentleman like to come as well?

RÉDILLON: Me?

LUCIENNE: No, he doesn't care for paintings!

PONTAGNAC: Aha! …Right! *(About to leave)* It's annoying, having to leave them alone together. *(He exits up right.)*

(LUCIENNE, *to* RÉDILLON *who nervously paces back and forth:)*

LUCIENNE: Sit down, my dear.

RÉDILLON: *(At right)* Thanks, but I came in a cab, I can use the walk.

LUCIENNE: *(Going to the fireplace)* What's the matter with you?

RÉDILLON: Nothing! Do I look as if anything's the matter with me?

LUCIENNE: You look like a caged grizzly. Was it that gentleman's presence that makes you cross?

RÉDILLON: It makes no difference to me! If you think I give that gentleman a second thought!

LUCIENNE: I was under the impression…

RÉDILLON: Certainly not! …No way, no way, would I give the slightest thought… *(After a pause)* Who on earth is that man?

LUCIENNE: I thought you didn't give him a second thought!

RÉDILLON: Excuse me if I'm being indiscreet.

LUCIENNE: You're excused.

RÉDILLON: Most kind of you. *(After a pause)* Is he trying to seduce you?

LUCIENNE: Yes.

RÉDILLON: A fine thing!

LUCIENNE: Do you have a monopoly on seduction?

RÉDILLON: But it's different with me! *I* love you!

LUCIENNE: What if he says the same thing!

RÉDILLON: Be serious! A man you've known for only ten minutes.

LUCIENNE: Twenty!

RÉDILLON: Oh, ten, twenty, I'm not a time-clock.

LUCIENNE: And besides, although he was introduced to me twenty minutes ago, I've known him by sight much longer! He's been following me in the streets for a week.

RÉDILLON: No!

LUCIENNE: Yes!

RÉDILLON: Filthy swine!

LUCIENNE: *(In front of the fireplace)* Thank you, on his behalf!

RÉDILLON: And your husband thought it clever to introduce you to him!

(LUCIENNE smiles and shrugs in confirmation.)

RÉDILLON: That's charming! Really, these husbands! You'd think they do it on purpose to put their lives in danger.

LUCIENNE: Mind what you're saying, Rédillon!

RÉDILLON: I say what I think! And then, when what's bound to happen to them happens to them, they have the audacity to complain! After all, why does Vatelin have to introduce men into his household? ...Do we need any more? Isn't our little three-way relationship enough for him?

(RÉDILLON, *noticing that* LUCIENNE *is laughing:*)

RÉDILLON: It's true. I can't stand to see a man come near you, it drives me stark raving mad. *(One knee on the hassock)* But I can't tell that to your husband!

LUCIENNE: *(Going to him)* Now, now, calm down!

RÉDILLON: *(Weeping)* Oh, what's worse, I knew something terrible would happen to me today.

(LUCIENNE *and* RÉDILLON *come downstage.*)

RÉDILLON: I dreamed that all my teeth fell out...that I'd already lost forty-five of them, and when I dream of falling teeth, it never fails! The last time, somebody stole a little bitch I was fond of, and today they're trying to steal my mistress.

LUCIENNE: Your mistress! But I'm not your mistress.

RÉDILLON: You're the mistress of my heart...nobody, not even you, can prevent that.

LUCIENNE: Just so long as you relieve *me* of the responsibility!

RÉDILLON: Swear to me that you will never love that man.

LUCIENNE: That man? Why, you're out of your mind, my friend! …Do I know anything about him? Have I paid him the slightest attention?

RÉDILLON: Thanks. After all, you probably noticed how unattractive he is. Did you see his nose? …With a nose like that, it's impossible to love.

LUCIENNE: Ah!

RÉDILLON: Whereas, *I've* got the nose that's needed! I have a nose made for love, a loving nose!…

LUCIENNE: How do you know?

RÉDILLON: I've been told so.

LUCIENNE: Ah. I see.

RÉDILLON: Ah, Lucienne, don't forget that you promised me you would never be anyone's but mine!

LUCIENNE: *(Correcting him)* Excuse me! If ever I were to be anyone's! But for that to happen, my poor friend, we need very special circumstances! *(She sits at the right of the desk.)*

RÉDILLON: *(Sighing)* Ah! Yes, your husband has to cheat on you first! And then! *(Aside)* What on earth is the man waiting for? He has no passion, the mollusc! *(Aloud)* But don't you realize the cruelty of the torture you inflict? Like continually serving a man appetizers and never feeding him the main course!

LUCIENNE: Well, my poor friend…have dinner somewhere else!

RÉDILLON: I have to! What do you expect, I'm flesh and blood! But I'm hungry, I'm starved!…

LUCIENNE: Oh, you're so unattractive when you cry famine.

RÉDILLON: And you laugh, heartless creature! *(He sits on the hassock.)*

LUCIENNE: Would you rather I wept? Especially now that I know you've been snacking on the side. *(She stands.)*

RÉDILLON: Oh, they're something special, my snacks! You can have my snacks! If you were only willing, I'd do away with all my snacks! But you're not willing: so tough luck for you, others have the benefit.

LUCIENNE: *(Back to the desk)* Fine, and much good may it do them!

RÉDILLON: *(Conceited)* I can guarantee *that*!

LUCIENNE: *(Going back upstage)* And this is the man who was talking about his love!

RÉDILLON: Absolutely! What difference does this make? Is it my fault if, besides love, there's…there's… the beast in man!

LUCIENNE: True enough! I was rather surprised you hadn't mentioned it before! Well, can't you take it upon yourself to slay…the beast?

RÉDILLON: I could never hurt an animal.

LUCIENNE: Poor baby! Well then, keep it on a leash.

RÉDILLON: I do that all the time. However, the beast is too strong. It drags me around behind it. So, what do you expect? Since there's no other way, well, I resign myself to it. *(Rising)* I take the beast out for walks. *(He moves right.)*

LUCIENNE: Ah, men! Poor Ernest! And what is its name? *(She sits on the sofa.)*

RÉDILLON: Whose?

LUCIENNE: The beast you take for walks?

RÉDILLON: Puss-puss… short for Pussywillow.

LUCIENNE: Delightful!

RÉDILLON: *(Going to her)* Oh, but my heart plays no part in it, you know Puss-puss means nothing in my life! There's only one woman in my sights, only one, you! What matter the altar on which I sacrifice, if the burnt offering is intended for you!

LUCIENNE: Really! Most kind of you.

RÉDILLON: My body, my person may be with Puss-puss, but my thoughts fly to you! ...My arms enfold her, but I make believe I'm holding you in my embrace! I tell her, "Keep still! I don't want to hear your voice." I close my eyes and call her Lucienne.

LUCIENNE: But that's identity theft! I won't have it! And she goes along with this?

RÉDILLON: Puss-puss? Very nicely! She even thinks she's supposed to do the same thing! She closes her eyes and calls me Clément.

LUCIENNE: *(Rising and crossing upstage)* Oh, that's exquisite! It sounds like a play performed by stand-ins.

RÉDILLON: *(In a burst of passion)* Oh, Lucienne, Lucienne, when will you put an end to the torment I endure? When will you say to me, "Rédillon, I am yours! Do with me what you will!"

LUCIENNE: Eh? What are you doing?

RÉDILLON: *(Kneeling before her)* Ah! Lucienne, Lucienne, I love you...

LUCIENNE: Will you get up! ...My husband may come in! Twice already he's caught you on your knees to me like this!

RÉDILLON: I don't care! Let him come in! Let him see me!

LUCIENNE: Certainly not! I won't have it! What an idea!

(LUCIENNE pushes RÉDILLON away. He falls back seated on the floor. She moves away and sits at the desk.)

RÉDILLON: What was I saying just now, dear lady?

(VATELIN *and* PONTAGNAC *enter.*)

VATELIN: *(Stopping when he sees* RÉDILLON *on the ground)*
Oh fine! There you are on the floor again.

RÉDILLON: As you can see... Uh! How are you?

VATELIN: All right, thanks. Is this an obsession or what?
(To PONTAGNAC.*)* You wouldn't believe it, my dear
fellow. Oh, this is my friend Rédillon. *(Introducing)*
Monsieur Rédillon, Monsieur Pontagnac.

PONTAGNAC: Don't bother, we've met already.

VATELIN: Ah?... It's the only position I ever see him in.
Every time he waits for me in the drawing-room—and
it's not that there aren't chairs—I can't come in without
finding him sitting on the floor.

PONTAGNAC: *(Drily)* Indeed!

RÉDILLON: I'll tell you what it is! ...It's a childhood
habit, I liked to roll around a lot. So, every time I pay a
call, instead of standing up...

VATELIN: What an absurd habit! That's ridiculous.
Your mother must have been frightened by a carpet
sweeper!

RÉDILLON: *(Rising)* Ha ha ha! Very funny, very funny!

LUCIENNE: *(Who has risen)* Well, did you admire my
husband's paintings, Monsieur Pontagnac?

VATELIN: I should think so! He was in seventh heaven!
He said, "The museums haven't got anything like
that!" *(To* PONTAGNAC*)* Right?

PONTAGNAC: Yes, yes, yes. *(Aside)* Luckily for them!

(Doorbell rings.)

VATELIN: *(Indicating offstage left)* Wait! I have some
more in there...if you'd like?...

PONTAGNAC: No, no! Not so many delights on one day. I'd prefer to save them for another time.

VATELIN: Ah, it's a shame that poor Madame Pontagnac is in bad health. I'd be proud to show her my picture gallery.

PONTAGNAC: Ah, what can you do…her rheumatism… on the Riviera.

VATELIN: The little cart, yes, yes! Ah! poor human frailty!

ALL: *(With a sigh)* Ah, yes.

JEAN: *(Enters at back and announces)* Madame Pontagnac!

ALL: Huh!

PONTAGNAC: *(Leaping; aside)* Son of a gun of a bitch! My wife!

ALL: Your wife!

PONTAGNAC: Uh! Yes…no…I guess so!…

LUCIENNE: I thought she was on the Riviera!

VATELIN: That's right, for her rheumatism.

PONTAGNAC: Yes, well, I don't know! …Maybe she's been cured!… *(To JEAN)* We're not at home! …Tell her we're not at home!

LUCIENNE: By no means! On the contrary! Show her in.

(JEAN exits.)

PONTAGNAC: Yes, just what I said, show her in!… *(Aside)* Oh my oh my oh my oh my oh my!

ALL: *(Aside)* What's wrong with him?

RÉDILLON: *(Aside)* The clown doesn't seem to be enjoying himself.

PONTAGNAC: *(Aside)* Now I'm really in for it!… *(Aloud)* I beg of you, my friends, Madame, for reasons I shall explain later, if my wife questions you, not a word. Or rather, say what I say! eh? Say what I say!

CLOTILDE: *(Entering)* I beg your pardon, gentlemen, Madame...

PONTAGNAC: *(Running up to her)* Ah, there you are, darling! What a wonderful surprise! ...I was just leaving! So say good-bye to the lady and gentlemen, and let's go. Come on, let's go!

ALL: Huh!

CLOTILDE: Certainly not. What an idea!

PONTAGNAC: Yes, yes!

CLOTILDE: No, no!

LUCIENNE: Leave her alone!

PONTAGNAC: All right, all right! I'll leave her alone! *(Aside)* Good grief! Good grief!

(CLOTILDE, sitting on a chair offered her by VATELIN:)

CLOTILDE: Excuse me for dropping in on you, Madame, before I had the honor of your acquaintance.

LUCIENNE: *(Seated)* On the contrary, Madame, I'm the one who...

VATELIN: *(One knee on the hassock)* Forget it...it doesn't matter...

CLOTILDE: But my husband's been talking about you for such a long time...

VATELIN: Really? ...Ah, that's nice of Pontagnac.

CLOTILDE: ...So I finally made up my mind: "This state of affairs can't go—intimate friends whose wives have never met!"

LUCIENNE & VATELIN: Intimate!

CLOTILDE: Ah! If you knew how fond my husband is of you! Why, I almost got jealous! Every day the same

story: "Where are you off to?"… "To the Vatelins's."
And in the evening, "Where are you off to?"… "To the
Vatelins's." Always to the Vatelins's!

VATELIN: What do you mean, To the Vatelins's?

PONTAGNAC: Why, of course! How can you be so
surprised? *(Quickly, to* CLOTILDE*)* You haven't seen his
picture gallery yet, have you? Come and see his picture
gallery! It's well worth seeing, his picture gallery!

CLOTILDE: No, no, stop it! …What's the matter with
you?

PONTAGNAC: Me? Why, nothing! What do you mean?

VATELIN: I don't understand any of this…

RÉDILLON: *(Seated in the armchair, aside)* This is really
very funny, most amusing!…

CLOTILDE: You seem so upset! …Might it be because…

PONTAGNAC: Me? Where do you get "upset"? How am
I upset? I'm perfectly calm… However, you were about
to tell Monsieur and Madame Vatelin that I come and
visit them every day! But they know quite well that I
come and visit them every day.

LUCIENNE: *(Aside)* Aha!

VATELIN: *(Aside)* Ah, now I get it!

PONTAGNAC: *(To* VATELIN, *making signs to him)* Right,
Vatelin? Aren't you well aware that I come and visit
you every day?

VATELIN: Yes, yes, yes, yes, yes!

PONTAGNAC: There, you see!

RÉDILLON: *(Rising and intervening)* I've even run into
him here.

PONTAGNAC: *(Stares at him in astonishment; aside)*
Huh!… *(Then in a whisper)* Thank you, Monsieur!

RÉDILLON: *(In an undertone)* Don't mention it. *(He sits down again.)*

PONTAGNAC: Well, are you satisfied now?

CLOTILDE: *(Doubtful, rises)* Yes, yes, yes. *(She moves a bit left.)*

PONTAGNAC: Well then!

VATELIN: *(Aside)* Poor Pontagnac, this really hurts me! *(Undertone to* PONTAGNAC*)* Wait, I'll get you out of this!

PONTAGNAC: Good!

VATELIN: As a matter of fact, Madame, my friend Pontagnac, in the course of his frequent visits, has often spoken of you.

CLOTILDE: Oh, really!

PONTAGNAC: *(Undertone)* That's it! Excellent!

VATELIN: And I should have asked to be introduced to you a long time ago, had I not known you were on the Riviera!

CLOTILDE: The Riviera!

PONTAGNAC: *(Aside)* Uh-oh! *(Aloud, spinning* VATELIN *around so that he can get between* VATELIN *and* CLOTILDE.*)* No, no! What Riviera? What's the Riviera go to do with it? How did the Riviera get into this?

VATELIN: What do you mean, how…?

PONTAGNAC: Of course, of course! Whoever brought up the Riviera?

VATELIN: *(Trying to undo it)* No, Riviera! …I said, "Riviera" …I meant: had I not known you were…you were…

PONTAGNAC: Nowhere at all!

VATELIN: *(Totally confused)* That's right, had I not known you were nowhere at all!

PONTAGNAC: Fine, fine! *(Undertone)* Keep your mouth shut!

VATELIN: That's all right with me! I don't know *what* I'm saying anymore!

(VATELIN and PONTAGNAC go upstage.)

RÉDILLON: *(Aside)* Two's company, three's a disaster.

CLOTILDE: *(Aside)* I'm definitely beginning to believe my suspicions were not unfounded. *(Aloud)* Please, Monsieur Vatelin, don't apologize! I knew not to expect your visit, for my husband had informed me of your state of health!

PONTAGNAC: *(Aside)* Here we go again!

VATELIN: My state of health?

CLOTILDE: Why yes, bedridden with rheumatism.

VATELIN: No, that's you!

CLOTILDE: Me? No, it's you!

PONTAGNAC: *(Going to VATELIN)* Yes, it *is* you! You don't have to deny it for your wife's sake.

VATELIN: Ah! It is me! …Fine, fine! …All right, it's me too.

PONTAGNAC: No, not you *too*! *(Dragging VATELIN left)* Listen, take me to see your picture gallery! …I haven't seen all of it! …Not all of it!

VATELIN: Ah! With pleasure! Let's go look at the gallery!

CLOTILDE: Edmond, are you leaving?

(LUCIENNE rises.)

PONTAGNAC: Wait here, I'll be right back! Right back!

VATELIN: We'll be right back! Right back!

(PONTAGNAC and VATELIN exit left.)

CLOTILDE: Oh, this is too much! Come now, Madame. Be frank with me. Am I being hoodwinked?

LUCIENNE: Yes, you are, Madame!

(CLOTILDE *falls into the chair near the hassock.*)

LUCIENNE: Since our husbands stick together so closely—being men—I suppose we women ought to show a little solidarity! Yes, you are being hoodwinked! *(She sits.)*

CLOTILDE: I thought so!

LUCIENNE: Your husband is not my husband's most intimate friend, fellow club member, etc., etc.! He never set foot in this house until today, and if you *did* find him here this afternoon, please realize it that it was not because he was visiting a close friend, but because he followed a woman into her drawing-room.

CLOTILDE: A woman!

LUCIENNE: Yes, me!

CLOTILDE: No!

LUCIENNE: After he followed me in the street with what I might call the persistence of a ...

RÉDILLON: *(In his armchair)* Skunk!

CLOTILDE: Yes indeed!

LUCIENNE: He discovered to his intense disappointment that the woman was the wife of a friend of his. Out of luck! ...In any case, your husband lied to you, and as to his alleged visits here, they were merely an alibi to conceal his escapades.

CLOTILDE: The swine!

RÉDILLON: You took the words right out of my mouth!

LUCIENNE: *(Rising)* Please forgive me, Madame, for speaking out so crudely. But you appealed to me to be frank, and I have given you a frank explanation!

CLOTILDE: *(Rising)* You've done the right thing, Madame, and I thank you for it.

LUCIENNE: Anyhow, I acted towards you the way I should like someone to act towards me, if ever my husband…

RÉDILLON: *(Disappointed)* Ha! …Not a chance!

LUCIENNE: Fortunately, you ought to say!

CLOTILDE: Ah! I see my way clear now, my suspicions were well founded! Oh, now I've learned what I needed to know! On guard, Monsieur Pontagnac! I'll go undercover, spy on you, let you off the leash, catch you in the act, and then!… *(She crosses downstage.)*

LUCIENNE: Then what?

CLOTILDE: *(Picking up the chair and carrying it up to the sofa)* Ha, ha, ha! Do I have to spell it out?

LUCIENNE: An eye for an eye?

CLOTILDE: Exactly!

RÉDILLON: *(Rising)* Bravo!

LUCIENNE: *(Growing heated along with* CLOTILDE*)* Ah! same as me! If ever my husband!…

RÉDILLON: I know, I know!

CLOTILDE: After all, I'm young, I'm attractive.

LUCIENNE: So am I.

CLOTILDE: What I'm saying may not be modest…

RÉDILLON: Never mind, when you're angry you don't have to be modest!

CLOTILDE: In any case, I could find more than one man who'd be delighted to…

RÉDILLON: You don't say so!

LUCIENNE: And so could I! Right, Rédillon?

RÉDILLON: I'll say!

CLOTILDE: And I wouldn't even bother to choose! Not even that! I feel it would prevent me from fully savoring my revenge! No, anyone at all, the first imbecile who came along!

RÉDILLON: Good idea!

CLOTILDE: *(To* RÉDILLON*)* You! If you'd like to. *(She crosses upstage.)*

RÉDILLON: Me? Ah, Madame...

LUCIENNE: Why not? And me too!

RÉDILLON: Ah, Lucienne!

CLOTILDE: *(Coming back downstage)* Very well! May I have your name and address?

RÉDILLON: Ernest Rédillon, 17 Rue Caumartin.

CLOTILDE: Rédillon, 17 Rue Caumartin. Fine! All right, Monsieur Rédillon, when I nab my husband, I'll run to you and say "Monsieur Rédillon, take me, I'm yours!" *(She falls into his arms.)*

LUCIENNE: *(Does the same thing)* And so will I, Rédillon! Yours! Yours!

RÉDILLON: *(Holding both women)* Ah! Ladies!... *(Aside)* My luck is amazing—conditionally.

(Sound of voices)

CLOTILDE: Our husbands! Not a word!

*(*VATELIN *and* PONTAGNAC *linger, downcast and hesitant, in the doorway.)*

CLOTILDE: Come in, gentlemen! Why stand in the doorway?

VATELIN: No reason! None at all!

CLOTILDE: Well, did you peruse the picture gallery? Were you pleased with it?

PONTAGNAC: Delighted, delighted! *(Aside, reassured)* Madame Vatelin didn't spill the beans! *(Aloud)* There are a few canvasses in particular... Ah! such canvasses! Close relations to the masters...

VATELIN: Think so?

PONTAGNAC: Among other, a stepson of Corot and a distant cousin of Millet. Really, why bother owning the masters themselves?

VATELIN: That's what I say. They're as well painted, and most of the time in better condition.

RÉDILLON: And much less expensive.

CLOTILDE: Well, in the meantime we were getting acquainted with Madame Vatelin. We spoke of you a good deal.

PONTAGNAC: *(Worried)* Oh?

CLOTILDE: And this gentleman told me he's often run into you here and thinks highly of you.

PONTAGNAC: No? He really said that? *(To RÉDILLON)* Ah, Monsieur! *(Aside)* And I thought... *(Aloud)* My dear Clotilde...Monsieur Pinkillon.

RÉDILLON: Red! Red!

PONTAGNAC: Sorry! ...Rédillon! ...Oh, red, pink... it's the same thing. Monsieur Rédillon, Madame Pontagnac.

CLOTILDE: We have already been introduced! *(She goes upstage with LUCIENNE, above the desk.)*

PONTAGNAC: Really? Splendid!... *(To RÉDILLON)* Dear sir, my wife is at home every Friday, if you would do us the honor...

RÉDILLON: How's that! *(Aside)* I get it: just now, when he was the seducer, he gave me the cold shoulder. His wife shows up, the husband in him rises to the surface, and he invites me home! All husbands are asking for it!

JEAN: *(Enters)* There is a lady asking for the master.

VATELIN: *(Going upstage and replacing the chair)* For me? Who is she?

JEAN: I don't know. It's the first time I've seen the lady.

LUCIENNE: A lady! What does she want?

VATELIN: *(With an "I dunno" gesture)* Who knows, my dear!... *(To JEAN)* Did you ask her name?

LUCIENNE: *(To JEAN)* Is she pretty?

JEAN: *(Making a face)* Pfutt!

VATELIN: Never you mind, Jean! Please, my dear, don't ask the servant to pass judgment on the people who come to see me. *(To JEAN)* Did you say I was in?

JEAN: Yes, the lady is waiting in the parlor.

VATELIN: All right, let her wait. I'll see her shortly.

(JEAN exits at the back.)

CLOTILDE: I see you have business, Monsieur Vatelin. I shan't take up any more of your time...especially when you're receiving a lady.

VATELIN: Oh, some client or other! ...It's not urgent! She's obviously not here to see the man, but the lawyer.

LUCIENNE: I should hope so.

CLOTILDE: Good-bye, dear lady! ...Most pleasant, Monsieur...uh...

PONTAGNAC: Rédillon!

RÉDILLON: 17, Rue Caumartin, exactly.

CLOTILDE: That's right. *(To PONTAGNAC)* Remember that, my love!

RÉDILLON: Oh, it's in the phone book!...

PONTAGNAC: Makes no difference, I always write things down.

RÉDILLON: In any case, I'll come downstairs with you. I have a few errands to run. *(To* LUCIENNE*)* Good-bye, Madame. *(Undertone)* Good-bye, dearest Lucienne!... *(To* VATELIN*)* Good-bye, you!

PONTAGNAC: Well, let's be off... *(He shakes* VATELIN's *hand, then* LUCIENNE's.) Madame! *(Undertone, swiftly)* I'll leave my wife at home and come back to explain my behavior.

CLOTILDE: Coming?

PONTAGNAC: Right away! Right away!

CLOTILDE: *(Aside)* And keep on the straight and narrow, man!

*(*CLOTILDE *and* PONTAGNAC *leave.)*

VATELIN: Do you mind stepping out, darling, until I've dealt with this person... *(So saying, he rings.)*

LUCIENNE: Very well!... See you soon, Crispin dear. *(She exits left, carrying off her hat.)*

JEAN: *(Enters)* Did Monsieur ring?

VATELIN: Yes, show the lady in.

*(*JEAN *shows in* LIESL *through the entrance up right, then withdraws.)*

VATELIN: *(Seated at his desk, arranging papers to appear busy; not looking at her)* Won't you take a seat, Madame...

LIESL: *(Coming up behind him and giving him two sloppy kisses on the eyes)* Ach! Mein Liebling!

VATELIN: *(Horrified, rising)* Huh! What's this! *(Recognizing* LIESL*)* Madame Soldignac! Liesl! You here!

LIESL: *(Thick German accent)* Meinzelf.

VATELIN: You! You here! But this is madness!

LIESL: For vhy?

VATELIN: Well, what about Vienna?

LIESL: I lefft it.

VATELIN: What about your husband?

LIESL: I him *mit* me brought! He for pizness to Baris comes!

VATELIN: *(Falling into his chair)* Wonderful! ...But what are you doing here?

LIESL: *Was?* Vot I am doink *hier? Ach! Undankbarer! Ach! Du Bōsewicht, wie konnt du mich fragen warum ich hergekommen bin? Der ist ein Mann, für wen ich alles aufgegeben habe, meine Pflichten als Frau, meine eheliche Treue....* (Ach! Ingrate! Ach, you villain, how can you ask why I've come? This is the man for whom I've given up everything, my wifely duties, my marital fidelity...)

VATELIN: *(Rising and trying to interrupt)* Yes...yes... *(He goes to listen at his wife's door.)*

LIESL: *(Crossing to the right) Ich verlasse Wien! Ich überquere Europa! Alles um ihn zu reichen, and wenn ich ihn endlich finde, er fragt mich warum ich hier gekommen sei!* [Translation *(not spoken)*: I leave Vienna. I cross Europe. Everything to reach him, and when I arrive, he asks me why I've come!]

VATELIN: *(Coming back down)* Yes! ...But that's beside the point! You keep talking German, and I don't understand a word of it! How did you get here? Why? What do you want?

LIESL: *(Behind the desk)* Vot I vandt? He asks vot I vandt! Vy, I vandt...you!

VATELIN: Me!

LIESL: *Ach, ja!* Pecauze ich luff you alvays, me! *Ach!*
Weh! For you to findt, I leaf Vienna, I grosst der
Kontinent by ein drain vitch ferry zick made me…I
trew…I trew…how you zay it?

VATELIN: Yes, yes, I get it! Then what?…

LIESL: *Nein,* I trew *up,* but it makes to me I don't care!
…I zay: I'm goink to zee him…*und* I am here, for *ein*
veek. *(She sits.)*

VATELIN: *(Falling on to a seat)* A week! Seven days! …
You're here for a week!

LIESL: *Ach ja,* a veek whole for you… *Ach!* Dell me dot
you luff me shtill! …Vhy to *mein* letters did you not
answer…I vas shtartink to dink: "*Ach, mein* Grispy,
he luffs me no more!…" *Ach ja,* you do luff me! …Oh,
Grispy! *Sagst mir dass du hast mich lieb!* [*Translation (not
spoken):* Tell me you love me!]

VATELIN: *(Rising)* Of course, of course!

LIESL: *(Rising and coming downstage)* Ven I am arrifed
dis mornink, I to you right avay wrote…und denn…
und denn…I zent not de letter…I zaid to meinzelf
maype he don't answer to me…I trew mein letter in de
vaste-paper blanket…und I took a *gut*-looking cab…
how you say…a hansom cab to gum here… Ach! How
it vas *schwer*…the adtress of you to findt…*Ich weiss
nicht,* der trifer don't untershtandink vrentch…he don't
vant to trife me.

VATELIN: *(Aside)* Good for the driver!

LIESL: I to him zaid, "Trifer, go Roo Tremol". He zays
back: Nefer heard from it…

VATELIN: Rue Tremol! …Now if you'd simply said, Rue
la Trémoille…

LIESL: Dot's vot I zaid: Roo Tremol.

VATELIN: That's what I mean.

LIESL: *Ach!* Grispy, Grispy, how I am happy! ...You come to fizit me dis night, *nicht wahr?*

VATELIN: Eh? Excuse me, excuse me...

LIESL: *Ach!* Don't zay *nein!* I foundt dis mornink a little groundt-vloor vlat, all vurnisht like I zay to you in de letter dot I put in de vaste-paper blanket... vorty-aid roo Rockypain.

VATELIN: You're staying on Rue Roquépine?

LIESL: *Ach, nein!* Vit mein husband at the Hotel Metropole, *aber* de groundt-vloor iss vor de two from *us.* I rended it *und* you kommt dis efenink, *ja!*

VATELIN: *(Pulling free and crossing down left of center)* Me! Oh no! Not likely!

LIESL: *Nein?* Vot for *nein?*

VATELIN: Because...because it's out of the question... Am I a free man? I have a wife! I'm married!

LIESL: You, you are marriedt?

VATELIN: Well, yes.

LIESL: *Ach!* In Vienna, you zed you vass a video.

VATELIN: What do you mean, a video? A widower.

LIESL: *Ach!* Video, vidover, it's de zame ding.

VATELIN: No, it's not the same thing! Not by a long shot!

LIESL: Vell, vot for did you dell me zo?...

VATELIN: Well, yes, I was a widower, because I'd left my wife in Paris... it's a figure of speech.

LIESL: Zo...zo...*was?* Ve iss ofer togedder?

VATELIN: Now, now, Liesl, be reasonable.

LIESL: Und you luff me no more... no neffer?

VATELIN: Yes, I will—next time I come to Vienna! All right?

LIESL: *(Bursting into tears and moving down left of center)* Ach! Grispy don't luff me no more! Grispy don't luff me no more!

VATELIN: *(Running to* LUCIENNE's *door)* Keep quiet, my wife may hear you.

LIESL: I don't gare!

VATELIN: *(Coming downstage)* But I do! Look here! I beg of you, a little self-control! I'm very touched, of course, but after all, that whirlwind romance in Vienna couldn't have lasted forever. Remember: we met on the train, you got sick from the rocking back and forth, I got sick, our two stomachs were so upset that our hearts thought they had something in common too. In Vienna you came to see me at my hotel every day, I met your husband, we became friends and what was to happen—happened. Well, let's be content with memories of that happy time, without trying to recreate it. Besides, here in Paris, I haven't the right... abroad I have an excuse! There are some things you can do on a detour that you can't do in the middle of the road! ...The whole continent was between me and my wife, but it isn't in Paris! ...Well, follow my example... learn self-denial! Like me! ...Forget me! There are other men as handsome as I am in Vienna.

LIESL: *Ach, nein, nein*! I gouldn't! ...*Ich bin* a fateful *Frau*. I hadt *ein* luffer, I don't take no odders!

VATELIN: All right then, be faithful... it's fine up to a certain point... but what about... your husband?

LIESL: Vell, I haff shtill de zame vun!

VATELIN: That's nice!

LIESL: *Nein, nein*! Vun only huzbandt, vun only luffer!...

VATELIN: Fine, fine! So long as you stick to your principles!

LIESL: *(Abruptly)* Zo, Grispy...Grispy! ...You vant me no more?

VATELIN: But don't you realize...?

LIESL: *Also!* ... Goot-bye, Grispy!

VATELIN: *(Going to open the door at back)* Good-bye, dear lady, good-bye! This way, please!

LIESL: *(Falling on to a seat)* Ach! I zuzpected dis ding. Ven I got no answers to *mein* letters... *so* I brebared a note for *mein* huzbandt. I vill to him zendt it.

VATELIN: Aha!

LIESL: *(Pulling out a letter and reading it)* "Lebwohl, Geliebster, vergiss mich. Ich bin bloss eine schuldhafte Frau, die jetzt nicht als den Tod zu erwarten hat. Ich bin die Geliebte des Herrn Vatelin gewesen, acht-undt-zwanzig Tremol Strasse, der mich verlassen hat, und jetzt werde ich Selbstmord begehen!" [Translation (not spoken): Farewell! Beloved, forget me! I am just a guilty wife who has nothing to hope for but death. I have been the lover of Monsieur Vatelin, 28 rue Tremol, who has abandoned me and so I commit suicide.]*

VATELIN: Well, that seems clear enough! Send it to him! ...Incidentally, what does it mean?

LIESL: You don't undershtandt it? *Ach!...* *(Translating)* Farevell, mein dear, vorget me! I am only a kilty voman who hass nottink to do but die!

VATELIN: Huh!

LIESL: I voss *die* mistress of Herr Vatelin, tventy-aid Roo Tremol...

VATELIN: What? Herr Vatelin? What an idea! ...and with my address attached!

LIESL: He trew me… He trew me… How you zay in Vrentch?

VATELIN: Up?

LIESL: *Nein,* ofer—*ja,* he trew me ofer… und I vill suizide meinzelf.

VATELIN: *(Coming down to her)* But that's insane! You don't intend to send him…

LIESL: *Ach ja!*

VATELIN: Never, you mustn't! …Kill yourself, you! And my name, my address…28, rue…

LIESL: Tremol…

VATELIN: Tremol, yes… Well! this is a nice kettle of fish! …Liesl! …My little Liesl!…

LIESL: *(Rising and crossing left)* Liddle Liesl iss ofer vit!

VATELIN: But that's sheer lunacy! Liesl, you wouldn't do such a thing!

LIESL: *Denn komm* tonighdt, vorty-aid, Roo Rockypain.

VATELIN: But I just told you I can't possibly. What pretext could I give my wife?

LIESL: *Nein?* Vell denn, I zuizide meinzelf.

VATELIN: Oh for heaven's sake! Well, all right, I'll come!

LIESL: *Ja? Ach! Hop-la!* Und you vill luff me again?

VATELIN: And I will luff you again, so there! *(Aside, furious)* Ugh!

LIESL: *Ach!* I am zo habby! Grispy, I luff you!

(Doorbell rings.)

VATELIN: *(Aside)* A regular barnacle! You couldn't stay in Vienna!

JEAN: *(Appearing at the back)* There's a gentleman asking if he can see Monsieur?

VATELIN: Who is it?

JEAN: Monsieur Soldignac.

LIESL: Mein huzbandt.

VATELIN: Him! *(To* JEAN*)* Yes, right away, I'll see him.

*(*JEAN *exits.)*

VATELIN: What do you suppose he wants?

LIESL: *Ich weiss nicht!* To shake your handt, vile he iss in Baris?

VATELIN: In any case, he mustn't see you! Here, let yourself out over there. *(He indicates the down right door and shows her through it.)*

LIESL: *Ja, das ist gut so!* Till diss efenink!

VATELIN: Yes, yes, agreed.

LIESL: Vorty-aid Roo Rockypain!

VATELIN: Roo Rockypain! Go on, go on!

LIESL: I'm goink on! I'm goink on! ...*Ach, du Bösewicht... ich liebe dich!* (Ah, you villain! I love you!) *(She exits right.)*

VATELIN: Oh, the results of a single misstep! ...To think that I cheated on my wife only once in our entire marriage...and that was excusable on account of the continent between us... Well! here's the result!...

LUCIENNE: *(Appearing left)* Has the lady gone?...

VATELIN: Yes, yes!

LUCIENNE: Who rang?

VATELIN: A friend I met in Vienna.

JEAN: *(Announcing)* Monsieur Soldignac! *(He exits.)*

SOLDIGNAC: *(Enters; slight German accent)* Ah! good afternoon, my dear friend, how are you?

VATELIN: *(Shaking hands)* Quite well. What a pleasant surprise!

(SOLDIGNAC bows to LUCIENNE.)

VATELIN: Dearest, Monsieur Soldignac!

LUCIENNE: Monsieur!

SOLDIGNAC: Madame, of course! Oh, very nice, very nice! *(Sitting.)* My dear friend, I can stay only a moment! I'm in a terrible hurry, you know. Some other evening, if you like, when I have the time, but today… business comes first…*Das Geschäft über alles*, as we say in German. *(Rising.)* So, first of all, I came to pay my respects, and next, on behalf of my wife…

VATELIN: *(Seated at the desk)* How is Frau Soldignac?

SOLDIGNAC: Very well, thank you. She gave me all sorts of messages… In fact, it's on her account that I'm here. My dear friend…I learned something new, you will be astonished: I am a two-timee…

VATELIN: A toot…what?

SOLDIGNAC: A two-timee. Frau Soldignac is two-timing me, if you prefer.

VATELIN: Eh?

LUCIENNE: *(Rising)* I beg your pardon. I'm afraid it would be indiscreet for me to stay.

SOLDIGNAC: Oh no, I don't mind. I'm very philosophical. However, I'm in a hurry, I have business to transact. *(Sitting down)* Now this morning I uncovered the whole mess…I found this letter in my wife's wastepaper basket.

VATELIN: *(Aside)* Great howling crashwagons! The letter she wrote to me. I hope she didn't mention my name…

SOLDIGNAC: *"Mein liebster…"*

VATELIN: *(Aside, somewhat reassured)* Liebster? …No, it's somebody named Liebster!

SOLDIGNAC: "I ham in Paris… now we will be able to luff each oder once more." You understand?

VATELIN: Yes, yes.

SOLDIGNAC: "This evening my husband"—that's me—"will be kept late on business. I ham alone, come for me, forty-aid, rue Rockypain, on the ground floor…I wait you! Liesl". What do you say to that?

VATELIN: Dear me, you know you mustn't leap to conclusions—at first sight. Maybe there's nothing to it.

SOLDIGNAC: *(Rising)* Don't be absurd! Well, we shall see! …Between two business meetings I went to the police…and this evening, I don't know who "Mein Liebster" is, but I'll nab the two of them, her and her "Liebster", Forty-aid, Roo Rockypain.

VATELIN: *(Aside)* Bloody hell! A good thing he warned me!

SOLDIGNAC: Won't I, Madame?

LUCIENNE: *(Rising)* Leave me out of it, Monsieur…

SOLDIGNAC: Yes, and then I divorce her.

VATELIN: *(Rising)* What, you want a divorce?

SOLDIGNAC: Yes indeed…only then shall I be satisfied. My wife is such a pest… She's always so passionate, and it disrupts my business. So I've come to you as a lawyer to draw up the papers for the divorce.

VATELIN: Me!

SOLDIGNAC: *(Going to pick up his hat at the back)* Yes, because I am in a hurry.

VATELIN: But it's no business of mine... how do you expect me to... you ought to do it in Vienna...

SOLDIGNAC: Why Vienna? I'm not from Vienna!

VATELIN: Ah?

SOLDIGNAC: *Nein! Ich bin aus* Marseille!

VATELIN & LUCIENNE: You!...

SOLDIGNAC: Quite so! Narcisse Soldignac, from Marseille, except that I was brought up as a child in Austria, where I went on living for business reasons, and where I was married, although at the French Embassy. Consequently you can draw up the papers.

VATELIN: Ah! So I have to...

SOLDIGNAC: Obviously, since I'm a Frenchman.

VATELIN: Yes, yes, yes... *(Aside)* Me...I'm the one who's got to... Ah! that's the limit!

SOLDIGNAC: Is it settled? ...Excuse me, but I'm in a hurry.

VATELIN: *(Aside)* Well, after all, what am I risking? *(Aloud)* It's settled, but only on one essential condition: you have to get the goods on your wife and her accomplice!

SOLDIGNAC: Of course, but I'll nab them this evening, 48, rue Rockypain.

VATELIN: *(Aside)* Yes, I'm not so dumb that you'll find us there.

SOLDIGNAC: And as for the gentleman, when I get my hands on him, I've reserved the pleasure of teaching him a little boxing lesson.

VATELIN: Ah, you're good at...

SOLDIGNAC: Me? Superb! ...So's my wife. I taught
her! ...Once I fought with the world's champion of
Vienna. Ah! I beat the bejesus out of him—as we say in
the South of France. He was punched so hard he flew
across the border.

LUCIENNE: Oh!

SOLDIGNAC: Indeed he did... that night by the first
train.

VATELIN: I see!

LUCIENNE: You have a very Marseille way of telling an
anecdote.

SOLDIGNAC: What else could it be? Even if I'm cynical
in the Viennese way, I still have the blood of the Midi
coursing through my veins... *(Rather lyrically)* Even in
the shadow of the snowy Alps, a tiny ray of southern
sunshine pierces through.

LUCIENNE: Oh, you're a poet.

SOLDIGNAC: *(His mood changing) Nein*, I have not the
time, I'm in a hurry... *Das Geschäft über alles,* as we
say in Vienna. Good-bye...and as for that gentleman
tonight... *(Making a boxing move.)* Take that! ...*Entre
nous!* as we say in Marseille.

*(SOLDIGNAC goes upstage and bumps into PONTAGNAC
coming in.)*

PONTAGNAC: Sorry!

SOLDIGNAC: Yes, good afternoon, Monsieur...I'm in a
hurry...

VATELIN: Pontagnac's just in time... *(To LUCIENNE)* Will
you see Monsieur Soldignac out? I have something to
ask Pontagnac.

LUCIENNE: *(Exits behind SOLDIGNAC)* Of course.

PONTAGNAC: Who in the world was that maniac?

VATELIN: Nobody, a Viennese from Marseille. You're right in the nick of time, my dear Pontagnac, I've a favor to ask you.

PONTAGNAC: Me?

VATELIN: Yes, man to man. I have a rendezvous with a lady this evening.

PONTAGNAC: You! Ah, you've destroyed my illusions.

VATELIN: That's how it is!

PONTAGNAC: So you're cheating on your wife?

VATELIN: There are occasional instances when a husband is compelled to…

PONTAGNAC: (*Delighted; aside*) He's cheating on his wife and he just told me!

VATELIN: Well, here's the problem… we planned to meet at a place where we mustn't set foot at the moment for peculiar but imperative reasons. You're an expert at this sort of thing: couldn't you suggest a hotel where I might…

PONTAGNAC: Of course, of course…The Continental, the Grand Hotel… Ah! and the Hotel Climax, my favorite spot. Very cosy, numerous exits!… But send a telegram so that they reserve you a room for this evening.

VATELIN: Thank you, my dear friend, thank you… I'll send the telegram this minute… and one to the lady to warn her and tell her to ask for the room in my name.

PONTAGNAC: That's right! That's right! But is your wife giving you a furlough for this evening?

VATELIN: Oh, that's no problem. My profession often obliges me to leave Paris. I'll tell her I was called away to the provinces to prove a will, an auction of the deceased's effects, something of the sort!

PONTAGNAC: Perfect! Perfect!

VATELIN: Excuse me, I'll go send the telegrams. *(He exits right.)*

PONTAGNAC: He's cheating on his wife! Oh bliss!

LUCIENNE: *(Returning at the back)* Funny sort, that Viennese.

PONTAGNAC: Ah, Lucienne! ...No, sorry...Madame! Come here quickly!

LUCIENNE: Well, what is it?

PONTAGNAC: Well, I... Oh, no, no, I can't!

LUCIENNE: Is that all?

PONTAGNAC: *(Aside)* Well, too bad, tough luck! ...After all, I don't owe Vatelin anything. He's no friend of mine, and, besides, love conquers all!...

LUCIENNE: Well?

PONTAGNAC: You gave your word, remember? You told me: "I shall never cheat on my husband until he cheats on me! But once he starts, I'll give him tit for tat without hesitation!"

LUCIENNE: Of course I said that!

PONTAGNAC: You swear you'll be true to your word, that you'll cheat on him as soon as you have proof!

LUCIENNE: Absolutely! On the spot!

PONTAGNAC: O rapture! Well then, I have that very proof! ...This evening, at the Hotel Climax, your husband will be with a woman...

LUCIENNE: No, no, you're lying!

PONTAGNAC: Am I? ...In a few seconds he'll tell you he just got a telegram, forcing him to go the provinces for a will or an auction.

LUCIENNE: Oh, that's impossible! Crispin! Him?

PONTAGNAC: Yes, Crispin in the flesh!

LUCIENNE: Is he capable of such a thing! Oh, if you can show me! Just show me!

PONTAGNAC: Well, this evening I'll spy on him when he leaves, immediately come back here for you and take you to the scene of the crime, the Hotel Climax. Willing?

LUCIENNE: *(Crossing left)* Am I willing! Am I!

PONTAGNAC: Here he comes! Easy now. *(He moves to the right.)*

VATELIN: *(Entering)* Oh, darling, there you are! I just had a nasty bit of news!

LUCIENNE: Oh, really! What is it?

PONTAGNAC: *(Aside)* Keep it up, pal, keep it up!

VATELIN: A telegram, just imagine, a telegram that obliges me to leave Paris this very evening by the 8 o'clock train.

LUCIENNE: *(Aside)* So it's true!

VATELIN: And go to Amiens to read a will.

LUCIENNE: The lowdown louse! *(Aloud)* But can't you send one of your clerks instead?

VATELIN: Oh no, impossible! …They insist that I officiate in person.

LUCIENNE: All right! Go ahead, my dear, go ahead! *Das Geschäft über alles,* as your Viennese puts it.

VATELIN: Quite so! This is really most annoying!

LUCIENNE: Hypocrite!

VATELIN: Please excuse me, telegrams to send! *(He exits right.)*

PONTAGNAC: Well! has the light dawned?

LUCIENNE: Oh! ...I see only too well... Oh! the swine! ...I thought he was one of the few faithful husbands, and now! Just like all the rest! All right, Monsieur Pontagnac, I shall wait for you tonight, and if I obtain proof that what you tell me is true, ah! I swear, I swear that one hour later...I shall be avenged!

PONTAGNAC: Thank you ever so much!... *(Aside)* What I'm doing may be a little underhanded... But then I have a good excuse. It's so I can sleep with his wife. *(Aloud)* Till tonight! *(He rapidly exits out the back.)*

LUCIENNE: *(Starting for her room)* Till tonight!

(Curtain)

END OF ACT ONE

ACT TWO

(Room 39 at the Hotel Climax. A large, comfortably furnished bedroom. At the back, a bed in an alcove. A table center. The entrance door is back left, opening on to a corridor. Down left, a door opening into Room 38. Upstage, a fireplace. Far up right a door to the washroom. Hotel-style furniture.)

(As the curtain rises, ARMANDINE, standing in front of the table center, is busy closing an overnight bag. There is a knock at the door at back.)

ARMANDINE: Come in.

(VICTOR, aged 17, dressed as a bellhop, enters.)

ARMANDINE: *(On seeing him)* Oh, it's you, kid! Well, did you run my errand?

VICTOR: Yes, Madame! The manager told me to tell Madame that he'd be right up.

ARMANDINE: Did you mention I wanted my room changed?

VICTOR: Yes indeed, Madame! He knew it already, the chambermaid told him.

ARMANDINE: Fine, thank you, bellhop. *(Aside)* The kid's cute. *(Aloud)* Say, come over here a minute.

VICTOR: Madame!

ARMANDINE: How old are you?

VICTOR: Seventeen.

ARMANDINE: Seventeen! You know, you're cute.

VICTOR: (*Blushing and looking at the floor*) Oh, Madame!

ARMANDINE: That make you blush? It looks like you enjoy it.

VICTOR: Oh! …Yes! …coming from Madame! (*He closes his eyes, not daring to say more.*)

ARMANDINE: (*Caressing his face*) Well, I won't take it back, you *are* cute!

(VICTOR, *just as* ARMANDINE's *hand is passing over his mouth, in a moment of frenzy seizes it with both hands and kisses it ardently.*)

ARMANDINE: Hey! What's all this!

VICTOR: Oh, excuse me, Madame!

ARMANDINE: You're not bothering me, kid!

VICTOR: Oh, Madame! I didn't know what I was doing. Did I hurt Madame?

ARMANDINE: (*Moving to the right*) Not much! …there are some impertinences that never hurt a woman.

VICTOR: I hope Madame won't tell the manager. It could get me fired!

ARMANDINE: (*Laughing*) Well, if I were mean. (*She sits on the sofa.*)

VICTOR: It's just that when I felt Madame's warm hand, so soft, on my cheek… I started to tremble all over, the room was spinning around! …Remember, Madame, I'm seventeen, and ever since I turned seventeen, I don't know…look, Madame, I've got pimples popping out… Yes, Madame, right here, I've got one starting on my neck. I showed it to a doctor who was leaving the hotel this morning, and he said, "My boy, you've contracted puberty!"

ARMANDINE: *(On the sofa)* Puberty! What in the world is puberty?

VICTOR: I don't know! But I think it means I'm old enough to make love… Ah! I can feel the sap rising in me.

ARMANDINE: Yes, yes, yes.

VICTOR: So when Madame came over like that… Oh! I hope Madame doesn't hold it against me?…

ARMANDINE: *(Rising)* Not at all! Not at all! and as proof, here's three francs.

VICTOR: *(Three francs in hand)* Three francs!

ARMANDINE: That's for you.

VICTOR: Oh, no, no, no! *(He puts them on the table.)*

ARMANDINE: Oh come on!…

VICTOR: And to think I'd give another seven francs to…

ARMANDINE: To?

VICTOR: *(Dumbfounded and holding back the sobs that build up in his throat)* To nothing, Madame! *(Changing his tone)* Here comes the manager, Madame. *(He runs upstage.)*

ARMANDINE: Poor baby! *(She picks up the three francs.)*

(VICTOR reaches the door and stands aside for the MANAGER, then exits.)

MANAGER: Did Madame send for me?

ARMANDINE: I did! About the room… to find out what's been done. *(She finishes packing her trunk and her bag.)*

MANAGER: Why, that was settled, Madame. We're giving you a different room—facing the street.

ARMANDINE: Fine. Because this one is depressing. *(Glancing at her trunk.)* And you understand, if I have to spend ten days here…while they redecorate my new apartment…

MANAGER: That's quite understandable, Madame.

ARMANDINE: Hell, I should think so! So if it's all the same to you…

MANAGER: By all means, Madame. As a matter of fact, if Madame had decided to keep her room, it would now be impossible to do so. It's just been taken!

ARMANDINE: Well, that's a stroke of luck. And who's the happy tenant?

MANAGER: A Monsieur Vatelin who telegraphed to reserve a room. So I reserved this one.

ARMANDINE: *(Closing her bag)* Vatelin, Vatelin… Nope! Don't know him! Well, never mind! Now what?… *(She sits left of the table.)*

MANAGER: Well, if it suits Madame, I shall let Madame have number 17? It faces the street.

ARMANDINE: So be it! If you say it's a good one… All I need is a cosy, comfortable room…that allows me to entertain a friend or two, and if he decides to stay the night…

MANAGER: Ah, Madame is not on her own, fine, fine, fine… Yes, yes, yes, I understand, Madame would like a room where, if need be… Why, then I'll let Madame have number 23… it will be much more suitable, it has twin beds!

ARMANDINE: Twin beds! What am I supposed to do with twin beds! Are you trying to make a fool of me?

MANAGER: What, Madame, but…

ARMANDINE: Really! Do you think I invite in spectators?

MANAGER: Oh, Madame! ...No, but I thought that for Monsieur, Madame's friend...

ARMANDINE: *(Rising)* The other bed's for him? Well, I can just see his face! No, no, I prefer number 17. *(She goes to close her trunk.)*

MANAGER: Very good, Madame.

ARMANDINE: See to it that my trunk is moved there!

MANAGER: Yes, Madame! *(He exits but stops on the outer threshold, speaking to someone we can't see.)* Monsieur?

(Sound of voices)

MANAGER: Yes, Monsieur, right this way, I'll see, Monsieur. *(He comes back downstage.)*

ARMANDINE: What is it?

MANAGER: A gentleman asking for Madame...

ARMANDINE: What gentleman?

MANAGER: I don't know! I'll ask him...

ARMANDINE: Oh, don't bother, show him in! And I'll be glad to see him!

MANAGER: Would Monsieur please come in!

(MANAGER steps aside to let RÉDILLON enter, and then exits.)

RÉDILLON: *(From the door)* Good afternoon!

ARMANDINE: You!

RÉDILLON: Me! *(He comes downstage and puts his hat on the mantelpiece.)*

ARMANDINE: Well really! ...My, my! How's about that!

RÉDILLON: Here I am in person!

ARMANDINE: And how've you been since last time?

RÉDILLON: Splendid! May I?

ARMANDINE: What?

(RÉDILLON *puckers up to show that he wants to kiss* ARMANDINE.)

ARMANDINE: All right!

(ARMANDINE *and* RÉDILLON *kiss on the lips.*)

RÉDILLON: Delicious!

ARMANDINE: So you *do* love me?

RÉDILLON: I adore you!

ARMANDINE: Well, you're not shy! ...What's your name again?

RÉDILLON: Ernest!

ARMANDINE: Ernest what? Have you got a last name? Didn't your father acknowledge you?

RÉDILLON: Yes, yes! Rédillon!

ARMANDINE: What a silly name!

RÉDILLON: Well, my family's been using it for so long...

ARMANDINE: Well, anyway, names don't make the man, do they? Look at me. You're good-looking, know that?

(RÉDILLON *makes a face.*)

ARMANDINE: You know what I think?

RÉDILLON: No.

ARMANDINE: You look like my lover!

RÉDILLON: Ah!

ARMANDINE: Anybody ever tell you that?

RÉDILLON: No! Who is your lover anyway?

ARMANDINE: (*Pushing him away*) What do you mean, who's my lover! He's a big shot, you know! ...Baron Schmitz-Mayer. (*She goes to sit on the sofa.*)

RÉDILLON: The banker? (*He sits down.*)

ARMANDINE: He's the Schmitz-Mayer who owns racehorses—oh, you must have heard about him. He's the one who made all that money with the forged stock issue... You know, the newspapers were full of it! The stuff's not worth a dime nowadays.

RÉDILLON: There's a lot of it around!

ARMANDINE: Well, his sister married the Duke...

RÉDILLON: Listen here, I didn't come to hear about your lover's family tree!

ARMANDINE: Poor guy! ...He's doing his military service at the moment, that's why he's not here.

RÉDILLON: Fine! All the better! ...Up the army! Up the army! *(Rising.)* Armandine baby!

ARMANDINE: What?

(RÉDILLON puckers up as before.)

ARMANDINE: *(Rising)* Ah! *(She gives him a lingering kiss.)* You know, I spotted you right away, giving me the glad eye yesterday at the theatre!

RÉDILLON: That so!

ARMANDINE: Weren't you in a box with Puss-puss?

RÉDILLON: Yes, you know her?

ARMANDINE: Do I know her! The way she knows me! By sight! She's a classy dame! In fact that's what got me interested in you. *(Coming down left)* Otherwise I wouldn't have responded to your winks, because normally I wait for an introduction...

RÉDILLON: Aha!

ARMANDINE: Well, what's the difference! A man with a classy dame isn't just anybody... It's intriguing! ... That's why I had the usher bring you my card during the intermission.

RÉDILLON: So I owe it all to Puss-puss...

ARMANDINE: Don't tell her! If we're going to…

RÉDILLON: Don't be silly!

ARMANDINE: Otherwise, nothing doing…because you know, I wouldn't want to do her dirt. *(She goes upstage to the fireplace.)*

RÉDILLON: *(Following her)* Don't worry! …You've got a great figure, you know… Does it all belong to you?

ARMANDINE: Hell! Who else should it belong to?

RÉDILLON: *(Taking her in his arms)* Why…me!… *(He kisses her.)*

ARMANDINE: Aha! Greedy! …But you'll let me have it back?

RÉDILLON: Of course.

ARMANDINE: Fine, because…guess who wouldn't like it otherwise? Schmitz-Mayer!

RÉDILLON: *(Leaving her and coming downstage)* Dammit! Will you stop taking about your Schmitz-Mayer!

ARMANDINE: *(Coming downstage)* Oh, but he's so much in love with me! …He's so funny! You know what he keeps telling me: "I love you because you're dumb!" You think I'm dumb?

RÉDILLON: No, you're not dumb! Armandine baby…

(ARMANDINE *and* RÉDILLON *kiss.*)

ARMANDINE: Oof! My little… How's it go again?

RÉDILLON: Ernest!

ARMANDINE: My little Ernest!

RÉDILLON: *(Sitting at left and pulling her on to his lap)* Come sit on my lap!

ARMANDINE: Oh! so soon!

RÉDILLON: Yes, so soon! …Oh, Lucienne! My Lucienne!

ARMANDINE: *(On his lap)* What Lucienne? My name's not Lucienne! It's Armandine!

RÉDILLON: *(In ecstasy)* No, Lucienne! Let me call you Lucienne! What do you care if I prefer that name? Ah, Lucienne!

ARMANDINE: You're pretty weird! ...Say, that reminds me, once this guy...

RÉDILLON: *(Still in ecstasy)* No, it doesn't remind you of anything! Shut up, don't say another word! And kiss me! Lucienne! My Lucienne! ...Is it you? Really you!...

ARMANDINE: No, it isn't.

RÉDILLON: Shut up! I wasn't asking for an answer! Ah, tell me it's you...

(A knock at the door)

ARMANDINE: Who's there?

RÉDILLON: *(Speaking over the voice behind the door, drowning it out)* Oh, Lucienne! My Lucienne!

ARMANDINE: *(To RÉDILLON)* Now it's your turn to shut up! I can't hear. *(To the door.)* Who is it?

VICTOR: *(Off)* Victor, Madame, the bellhop.

ARMANDINE: Oh, it's you! Come in!

VICTOR: *(Entering)* Madame, would it be possible... *(Scandalized at seeing ARMANDINE on RÉDILLON's lap)* Oh! *(Disappointed.)* Oh!

ARMANDINE: What's the matter, kid?

VICTOR: *(In a tender, gentle voice)* Madame, may we carry out the trunk now?

ARMANDINE: Yes, yes!

RÉDILLON: *(To VICTOR)* What trunk?

VICTOR: *(Brutally, to RÉDILLON)* This here trunk! Not the Pope's!

RÉDILLON: *(Rising and going to* VICTOR*)* See here! That's no way to answer me! I'll show you if it's the Pope's or not! This is unheard-of!

ARMANDINE: Oh, don't scold the poor kid, he's so cute!

RÉDILLON: I'm not talking to you! But I'll teach him to answer me politely.

ARMANDINE: Oh, it's not worth the trouble! Here, give him five francs!

RÉDILLON: What! After the way he…

ARMANDINE: Well, you can't stop me from giving him five francs! *(She sits at left.)*

RÉDILLON: The money is not the issue… Oh, all right! *(Holding out a five-franc coin to* VICTOR*.)* Here's five francs for this time, but don't let it happen again. *(He crosses right.)*

VICTOR: *(Flatly)* Thanks. *(Pocketing it; under his breath)* Pig!

RÉDILLON: *(Who hasn't heard)* That's just the way I am!

VICTOR: *(Tenderly to* ARMANDINE*)* Madame, I'll fetch the chambermaid to help move the trunk.

ARMANDINE: *(Seated left)* All right, go ahead, kid!

*(*VICTOR *exits.)*

RÉDILLON: *(Grumbling)* At least he'll learn the cost of being rude to me.

ARMANDINE: Well, you mustn't hold it against the poor kid. He's feeling down right now, he's sick.

RÉDILLON: Some reason! I don't give a damn if he's sick!…

ARMANDINE: If you had what he's got!…

RÉDILLON: What's he got?

ARMANDINE: I'm not exactly sure! I think he's got puberty!

RÉDILLON: Puberty! What do you mean, puberty?

ARMANDINE: *(Leaning on the chair arm)* That's right! That's what the doctor told him!

RÉDILLON: Is that his ailment? ...Well, maybe I do feel sorry for him!

ARMANDINE: Is it serious?

RÉDILLON: Puberty? Yes indeed!

ARMANDINE: *(Suddenly rising)* I hope it isn't catching!

RÉDILLON: Oh no! Unfortunately! Otherwise, good Lord! The virus would be worth a fortune.

(VICTOR enters, followed by CLARA.)

VICTOR: *(To CLARA)* Come on, give me a hand!

CLARA: This the trunk?

VICTOR: Yes, we're taking it down to number 17... *(Returning to get the overnight bag)* Ah, the bag!

(CLARA and VICTOR carry off the trunk and the bag.)

RÉDILLON: *(Going to her)* What? Are you moving?

ARMANDINE: Yes, I don't care for this room. I asked for one facing the street.

RÉDILLON: I don't see any improvement in facing the street. Well, the new room will do just as well. Let's be off to the new room. *(He goes to get his hat from the mantelpiece.)*

ARMANDINE: Us? What for?

RÉDILLON: *(Coming downstage)* What do you mean, what for? *(Snidely)* Don't be coy.

ARMANDINE: Oh, no, no, my dear, no, not tonight!

RÉDILLON: I beg your pardon?

ARMANDINE: Don't mention it. *(Crossing right)* Impossible, awfully sorry.

RÉDILLON: Ah! you mean it! Well, you've got a nerve! But…no, really…you don't expect me to go away just like that…with my tail between my legs!

ARMANDINE: *(Back against the table)* But there's no other way! I'm expecting a friend at eleven!

RÉDILLON: *(Going to sit on the bed)* A friend! That's hardly a reason! What kind of a friend?

ARMANDINE: A gentleman from Vienna! You don't know him. Monsieur Soldignac. And besides, every time he comes to Paris…

RÉDILLON: Don't tell me! It's disgusting!

ARMANDINE: *(Crossing left)* Well, he's going to show up!

RÉDILLON: *(Rising and coming downstage)* Well, don't be here! I know, come to my house.

ARMANDINE: To your house?

RÉDILLON: *(Taking her by the arm. Byplay)* Well, yes, to my house! I have a house. Do you think I live under a railway embankment?

ARMANDINE: But what am I going to tell *him*?

RÉDILLON: Well, tell him that you had to watch by the bedside of your sick mother—it's as old as the hills and it always works.

ARMANDINE: Oh, that isn't very nice!

RÉDILLON: Yes it is, it's very nice indeed! Come on, put on your hat and I'll take you there.

ARMANDINE: *(Going to the mantelpiece, takes her hat)* It isn't very nice, but it's tempting!

(A knock at the door.)

RÉDILLON & ARMANDINE: Come in!

(The MANAGER *enters back left.)*

MANAGER: Pardon me, Monsieur, Madame, for disturbing you, but the out-of-towners who rented this room are here…and so…

ARMANDINE: *(Putting on her hat)* You'd like us to hightail it out of here.

MANAGER: Oh! I won't put it like that!

ARMANDINE: I'll just finish putting on my hat and then clear out. Ask the gentleman, Monsieur—what's his name?…

MANAGER: Vatelin!

RÉDILLON: Vatelin?

ARMANDINE: Yes, to grant me a minute.

RÉDILLON: What, Vatelin here! Aha! What a lucky chance! Show him in, I'd be delighted to shake his hand.

ARMANDINE: What, you know him?

RÉDILLON: Do I ever!

MANAGER: *(To* PINCHARD, *outside)* Would Monsieur please come in?

RÉDILLON: *(Going upstage)* Ah, the dear fellow!

*(*PINCHARD, *in full army doctor's uniform, enters followed by his wife.)*

RÉDILLON: *(On seeing* PINCHARD*)* Oh! sorry! *(Aside)* It's not the same one.

*(*MME PINCHARD *makes cringing little bows to* ARMANDINE *and* RÉDILLON.*)*

PINCHARD: Heartbroken, Madame, Monsieur, to dislodge you in this fashion… *(Aside)* Deuce take it, what a gorgeous female!

(PINCHARD *hands his bag to* MME PINCHARD *who puts it on the table and returns to her husband.*)

PINCHARD: *(Aloud)* But I wired to reserve a room in this hotel for tonight and as you see by this note: "Reserved for you room 39." This is indeed the one assigned to me.

ARMANDINE: *(Putting on her gloves)* No, Monsieur, I ought to apologize for still occupying it. We were just about to leave.

PINCHARD: I insist, Madame, take your time! I should be broken-hearted if I disturbed you in the slightest way. If it's big enough for two, it's big enough for four.

ARMANDINE: Oh, Monsieur, you're too chivalrous!

PINCHARD: Not at all, Madame. *(To* RÉDILLON*)* My compliments, Monsieur, you have a very pretty wife.

(RÉDILLON *bows, flattered.*)

PINCHARD: I'd gladly trade her for mine.

ARMANDINE & RÉDILLON: *(Astonished)* What!

(ARMANDINE *and* RÉDILLON *stare at* MME PINCHARD, *who keeps smiling and bowing.*)

PINCHARD: Oh! plain and simple, and I'm not afraid to say so to my wife's face.

RÉDILLON: What, she doesn't care?

PINCHARD: No, she doesn't hear. She's deaf as a post! *(He goes somewhat upstage.)*

ARMANDINE & RÉDILLON: Ah! *(They suppress their laughter.)*

MME PINCHARD: I beg you, Madame, don't trouble yourself on our account!

ARMANDINE: *(Thanking her)* That's exactly what your husband was kind enough to tell us.

MME PINCHARD: *(Who didn't understand)* Oh, not in the least, Madame, not in the least.

PINCHARD: Did you understand that?

RÉDILLON: No.

PINCHARD: Neither did I. Her answers are a little incoherent, but that's only because she didn't hear a word.

MME PINCHARD: *(Most pleasant)* And my husband as well.

PINCHARD: You see! But one has to get used to it! It's twenty-five years now, you understand! We were married twenty-five years ago today, and so we came to Paris to celebrate our anniversary. I'll take her to the Opera.

RÉDILLON: *(To* ARMANDINE*)* He's taking a deaf woman to the Opera! ...Probably for the intermissions! *(To* PINCHARD*)* To the Opera, tonight? *(He looks at his watch.)*

PINCHARD: Yes, it's a bit late, but since they're performing *La Favorita* followed by *Coppélia*, we don't intend to get there until the ballet. Because music gets on my nerves, and my wife prefers ballet! She can watch the dancing, it keeps her entertained—only she says it would be an improvement if it had music! *(Tapping her arm)* Isn't that right, Bunnykins?

MME PINCHARD: What?

PINCHARD: *(Thumbs in the pockets of his tunic and tapping his stomach with his fingers)* Don't you think ballets ought to have music?

MME PINCHARD: *(Who's been watching his hands)* Oh, much better! It's calmed down at the moment! It was only on the train that it was upset!

*(*RÉDILLON *and* ARMANDINE *stare at one another.)*

PINCHARD: Ah, yes! ...No, that's something else! She was talking about her stomach... She's subject to little gas attacks, and it's better now. Well, all right! This is a little disjointed! ...Have to get used to it, have to get used to it!

ARMANDINE: Come, Monsieur, I don't wish to delay you any longer! Are you ready, Ernest? *(To* PINCHARD*)* Monsieur! *(She bows and goes upstage to the fireplace.)*

PINCHARD: Enchanted, Madame! Delighted, Monsieur.

RÉDILLON: Monsieur, the pleasure is all mine! I just wanted to mention one thing...

PINCHARD: What's that, Monsieur?

RÉDILLON: Can you imagine, Monsieur, my best friend is named Vatelin.

PINCHARD: *(Stupefied)* Ah!

RÉDILLON: Yes.

PINCHARD: Yes! ...Bless my soul, Monsieur, one confidence deserves another. *My* own best friend, Monsieur, is named Piedlouche!

RÉDILLON: *(Stupefied in turn)* Ah!

PINCHARD: Yes.

RÉDILLON: Yes! *(Aside)* What's that got to do with me?

*(*ARMANDINE *comes back downstage.)*

PINCHARD: Charmed, Monsieur! And thank you again, Monsieur.

RÉDILLON: Monsieur!

RÉDILLON & ARMANDINE: *(To* MME PINCHARD*)* Madame!

*(*MME PINCHARD *doesn't budge.)*

PINCHARD: *(Tapping his wife's arm)* Bunnykins!

*(*MME PINCHARD *turns to* PINCHARD*.)*

PINCHARD: Monsieur and Madame said Good-bye!

MME PINCHARD: I can't hear you!

PINCHARD: That's right! Wait! *(Simply moving his lips and not making a sound.)* Monsieur and Madame said Good-bye!

MME PINCHARD: Oh, sorry! Good-bye, Madame. Good-bye, Monsieur!

RÉDILLON: *(To* ARMANDINE*)* That's peculiar! ...She can hear only when we can't.

PINCHARD: That's right!

ARMANDINE: Coming, Ernest?

RÉDILLON: Coming!

*(*ARMANDINE *and* RÉDILLON *go a bit upstage.)*

(A knock at the door)

ALL: *(Except* MME PINCHARD*)* Come in!

VICTOR: *(Enters; to* ARMANDINE*)* Has Madame anything else to be moved?

ARMANDINE: No thanks, kid! Oh! let them know downstairs that if a gentleman asks for me, tell him I couldn't wait because I was called to my sick mother. Understand?

VICTOR: *(With a sigh)* Yes, Madame!

ARMANDINE: All right, kid! And get cured!

VICTOR: Thank you, Madame.

PINCHARD: Is he ill?

ARMANDINE: Yes, he has pimples! Take care of yourself! *(To* RÉDILLON*)* Come along!

*(*ARMANDINE, *about to leave, to* RÉDILLON *who's following her:)*

ARMANDINE: Ah, my bag!

RÉDILLON: Right! *(To* VICTOR*)* The bag, over there!

VICTOR: Here's the bag!

(He takes PINCHARD's *bag from the table and hands it to* RÉDILLON.*)*

RÉDILLON: *(Taking the bag, aside)* Is this the lady's bag? …Guess so!

(The PINCHARDs *are talking at right and don't see this byplay.* VICTOR, *sighing, watches* ARMANDINE *as she and* RÉDILLON *exit with the bag.)*

MME PINCHARD: I'd better get ready if we're going to the Opera! *(She starts towards the washroom and enters it.)*

PINCHARD: All right. *(To* VICTOR*)* Well, why are you standing around like a fireplug, you goldbrick! *(He goes to tidy up before the mirror over the mantelpiece.)*

VICTOR: Monsieur?

PINCHARD: Yes, you, you with the pimple!

VICTOR: Yes, Monsieur! Oh, it's not so bad!

PINCHARD: That's what you think! As a surgeon major in the cavalry, I've often seen what it leads to! …Let's have a look! *(He returns right.)*

VICTOR: *(Coming downstage)* Yes, Major! I caught it…

PINCHARD: I'm not asking for any of your blather! Pull down your pants!

*(*MME PINCHARD *returns from the washroom.)*

VICTOR: Major?

PINCHARD: Don't you understand French? I said, pull down your pants!

VICTOR: *(Aghast)* But, Major…

PINCHARD: What? Does my wife embarrass you? Don't mind her, she's deaf!

VICTOR: Ah! all right! (*He lays his hand on his top fly-button, then hesitates.*)

PINCHARD: Well, what are you waiting for?

VICTOR: Oh dear! Major, what I mean to say is, if you're doing this out of curiosity, fine. But if it's on account of the pimple, it's on my neck!

PINCHARD: On your neck! What is this song-and-dance! A pimple on the neck! You think that's serious? You think that'll exempt you from the draft, a pimple on the neck? You want to be let off from cavalry drill for a pimple on the neck! (*Marching up to him and forcing him back upstage.*) I ought to knock the pimples *out* of you, you damned shagass! (*He places his képi on the mantelpiece.*)

VICTOR: But, Major…

PINCHARD: Go on, scram! Beat it and at the double!

VICTOR: Yes, Major! (*Aside, running off*) What a grouch!

PINCHARD: (*To his wife*) Have you ever heard of such a thing! For a pimple on the neck!

MME PINCHARD: At ten-thirty, dear, so you have just enough time.

PINCHARD: That's not what I said! I was talking about his pimple!

MME PINCHARD: Check the program, you'll find out!

PINCHARD: (*Leaving her*) Yes, good-night! I'll go get ready, where's the bag?

MME PINCHARD: What?

PINCHARD: (*Shouting*) Where's the bag? (*Moving his lips soundlessly*) Where's the bag?

MME PINCHARD: What do you mean, where's the bag! You were the one carrying it.

PINCHARD: *(Shouting)* I was carrying it! *(Tiny voice)* I was carrying it?

MME PINCHARD: Positively! Where did you put it?

PINCHARD: This is the limit! Where did I put it?

(A knock at the door)

PINCHARD: *(While searching)* Come in!

(PINCHARD looks under the table, MME PINCHARD under the armchair.)

CLARA: *(Entering at the back)* I came to turn down the bed. Are Monsieur and Madame looking for something?

PINCHARD: *(Not looking at CLARA)* Yes, an overnight bag. Damn me to hell if I know where I put it!

MME PINCHARD: *(To her husband)* Look here, maybe the little bellhop took it into the other room.

PINCHARD: You think so? Oh, I would have seen him! *(He enters the room at right.)*

CLARA: *(To MME PINCHARD)* Does Madame prefer pillows of feathers or horsehair? *(Silence from MME PINCHARD)* Does Madame prefer pillows of feathers or horsehair? *(As before)* What's the matter with her? She's away with the fairies! *(Standing directly in front of her)* Does Madame prefer...

MME PINCHARD: Ah! good evening, my dear! *(She crosses left.)*

CLARA: *(Follows her)* Uh! Good evening, Madam! I was asking Madame...

PINCHARD: *(Re-entering and looking for his bag)* Well, don't ask her anything, you're wasting your time. I must have left it downstairs at the desk. What do you want?

CLARA: Monsieur, I wanted to know...

PINCHARD: Deuce take it! What a pretty girl!

CLARA: Whether Monsieur and Madame prefer pillows of feathers or horsehair.

PINCHARD: By my billycan! You're something special!

CLARA: I was asking Monsieur…

PINCHARD: What would you like, feathers or horsehair—half of *your* pillow is what I'd prefer…

CLARA: *(Shocked)* But, Monsieur…

PINCHARD: What's your name?

CLARA: Well, what's yours, buster?

PINCHARD: *(Crossing left)* She's getting familiar! Ah, ah, she's getting familiar!

CLARA: *(Going back up to the bed)* Who said you could get so familiar with *me*? *(She starts making the bed.)*

PINCHARD: *(Going to her)* Well, don't get put out, my girl. *(Pinching her rear)* Ah, you're getting familiar!

CLARA: *(Pulling away)* Will you leave me alone, Monsieur! *(Calling)* Madame, Madame!

PINCHARD: Call her, go ahead and call her!

CLARA: *(To* MME PINCHARD*)* Will you please ask your husband to keep his hands to himself?

MME PINCHARD: In Paris? Yes, until tomorrow!

CLARA: Why, she's deaf!

PINCHARD: As a post! You're adorable! *(He kisses her.)*

CLARA: *(Dealing him a resounding slap)* Take that! *(She goes up right.)*

PINCHARD: Ow!

MME PINCHARD: *(Turning around)* Did you get it?

PINCHARD: *(Rubbing his cheek)* Yes, blast it!

CLARA: Would Monsieur like anything else?

PINCHARD: *(Moving right)* No! No, no thanks! *(Aside)* By my billycan, what a fist!

MME PINCHARD: You have a toothache?

PINCHARD: No, no, it's nothing! *(After a fresh try with CLARA. To CLARA)* You can tell them downstairs to bring up my bag. I must have left it at the desk. Make sure it's here when I get back. *(He takes his képi from the mantelpiece.)*

CLARA: Very good, Monsieur. *(She goes to the bed.)*

PINCHARD: *(To MME PINCHARD)* All right, come on, Bunnykins! *(Lips only.)* All right, come on!

MME PINCHARD: *(Rising)* Let's go, I'm ready!

PINCHARD: Come on! *(Going back upstage)* La Favorita must be over by now. *(He says this using only his lips.)*

MME PINCHARD: What is a "Favorita" anyway? *(He tells her using only his lips.)* Oh! I don't care for that kind of woman at all!...

PINCHARD: Such is life, Bunnykins, such is life.

(PINCHARD and MME PINCHARD exit.)

CLARA: *(Alone)* I hope I cooled off that army doctor's ardor! Him and his "one half of your pillow"! Does he think that if I wanted to misbehave, I'd have waited for him? No, really!...

PONTAGNAC: *(Opening the door at back halfway and sticking his head in. He is carrying a small package)* I was right, I did hear someone leave the room. Since Vatelin rented it for this evening, he ought to be here soon, so let's set up the gizmo. *(He starts to tiptoe to the door at left.)*

CLARA: Does Monsieur wish something?

PONTAGNAC: *(Aside)* Dammit, the maid!

CLARA: Does Monsieur wish something?

PONTAGNAC: *(Aloud)* I…uh? …What do I wish?

CLARA: Yes!

PONTAGNAC: To see…to see the King of the Belgians!

CLARA: He ain't here!

PONTAGNAC: Ah! He ain't here! …Darn it! …Well, I didn't suppose he would be…

CLARA: Then why…

PONTAGNAC: I was sure it was room 39, only I was wondering whether this is the right hotel? …There, you see, it ain't the hotel!

CLARA: Ah, well, Monsieur, if that's your only mistake.

PONTAGNAC: It's not my fault. When I saw the King today he said, "Old boy, we're staying at the Climax, I'm in room 39." So I was sure of the room. As for the Climax, who knows? What with his accent! I heard Climax, but he could have said Continental.

CLARA: Monsieur is an official of the Court…

PONTAGNAC: Yes, yes, just a bit, an insignificant little minister! So, you see, to be near him, I rented 38… *(Approaching the left door)* 38 over here.

CLARA: I know where it is.

PONTAGNAC: *(Up against the door, trying to remove the key from it)* Over here, number 38.

CLARA: I know! *(She goes to the bed.)*

PONTAGNAC: *(Who has made off with the key; aside)* There we go! I've got the key! *(Aloud)* If he's not here, he's not here. All or nothing, right? …Sorry to have disturbed you, Mademoiselle. *(He exits humming.)*

(CLARA, startled, watches him go.)

CLARA: *(Laughing)* Has he gone? Court official indeed! A fugitive from a police court, most likely.... Well, let's get the pillows. *(She exits at back.)*

(We hear a key turning in the lock to the door at left and PONTAGNAC, followed by LUCIENNE, slips in cautiously.)

PONTAGNAC: You can come in, there's no one here!

LUCIENNE: Is this the place?

PONTAGNAC: This is the place!

LUCIENNE: This room?

PONTAGNAC: Number 39. Exactly!

LUCIENNE: *(Sitting in the armchair)* How disgusting! ... And to think that it's in this room! ...And yet the room seems respectable enough! So deceptive! So it's in this room that my husband is about to...

PONTAGNAC: *(Removing his gloves)* With another woman!

LUCIENNE: *(Rising)* Yes! And then the two of them behaving in the intimate way he does with me...with his words, his caresses, his sweet nothings, and, and then? Oh! no, no, I can't, I won't! Oh Lord! Can *you* stand by in cold blood?

PONTAGNAC: Why not, if it's in a good cause?

LUCIENNE: *(Crossing right)* Shut up! I can see it only too clearly! I can imagine it only too vividly! Terrifying images rise up before my eyes! No, no, I won't look, I won't! *(She puts her hands over her eyes.)* But then, no, I'd rather keep my eyes open. When I close them, I can see it better still!

PONTAGNAC: For pity's sake, don't get so overwrought!

LUCIENNE: I feel as if I detest the very surroundings. *(She goes upstage, passing behind the sofa.)* The walls for their complicity, the furniture for being witness to this… Oh, no, no, I won't, I won't! The service bell, where's the service bell!

PONTAGNAC: *(Stopping her)* The service bell? What for?

LUCIENNE: I want them to remove the bed!

PONTAGNAC: Don't be ridiculous! …Do you want to ambush your husband, yes or no?

LUCIENNE: Yes, of course I do!

PONTAGNAC: Well then, if you want tangible evidence of the crime, don't remove the *modus operandi.*

LUCIENNE: This is awful, this ordeal you've forced on me.

(LUCIENNE and PONTAGNAC come a bit downstage.)

PONTAGNAC: We'll try not to protract it needlessly.

LUCIENNE: Good.

PONTAGNAC: So long as we show up at the critical moment.

LUCIENNE: Before, oh! before!

PONTAGNAC: Yes, what I mean is, not too soon to have to watch the tuning-up and not too late…

LUCIENNE: To miss the overture.

PONTAGNAC: That's right!

LUCIENNE: All right! But how will we know?…

PONTAGNAC: *(Going to the table)* Well, I've already taken that into consideration and this is my device! *(He places two electric buzzers wrapped in paper on the table and displays them.)*

LUCIENNE: What's that? Electric buzzers?

PONTAGNAC: Precisely! Have you ever heard of bell fishing?

LUCIENNE: No.

PONTAGNAC: Well, bell fishing is when you put a bell on the end of your line and the fish itself rings to alert the fisherman that he's been caught. That is the very procedure I intend to use on Vatelin.

LUCIENNE: You're going to fish for my husband with bells?

PONTAGNAC: That's right, he and his... companion will be kind enough to ring for us at the proper moment.

LUCIENNE: Don't be silly!

PONTAGNAC: Silly? Wait, you'll see how simple it is.

(PONTAGNAC, *going up to the bed, followed by* LUCIENNE:)

PONTAGNAC: What side does your husband usually sleep on?

LUCIENNE: The outside.

PONTAGNAC: The outside, fine! Consequently, the lady is on the inside! Outside, inside! Fine! That settled, I take these two electric buzzers! The bigger one, here! *(He rings one of the buzzers. Deep, sonorous tone)* We'll call this one Vatelin! And the other one. *(He rings the other buzzer. A shrill tone)* That's the lady! Fine! I place the gentleman here. *(He slips the first buzzer under the mattress, in the spot* LUCIENNE *indicated for her husband. Then he goes round the bed to the wall side.)* And the lady here! *(He slips the other buzzer under the other side of the mattress.)*

LUCIENNE: And then what?

PONTAGNAC: What do you mean, and then what? There we are, the trap is baited.

LUCIENNE: Baited?

PONTAGNAC: *(Behind the bed)* All we have to do is wait until the fish bites. One of them gets into bed. Ding dong, a bell rings! We don't budge, we've only caught the one. Suddenly the second bell joins the first, there we are! We've caught both of them! *(He comes out from behind the bed.)*

LUCIENNE: That's ingenious.

PONTAGNAC: Oh, no! merely brilliant, that's all!

(Sound of voices at the back)

PONTAGNAC: *(Picking up his hat and cane)* I hear someone, it may be our party. *(He goes up left.)*

LUCIENNE: Them! I'll tear their eyes out!

PONTAGNAC: *(Stopping her)* They've barely arrived and you want to tear their eyes out? Quick, come on, there's no time. *(He pushes her ahead of him.)*

LUCIENNE: *(As if to her husband)* You won't miss anything for having to wait!

(LUCIENNE and PONTAGNAC exit left and then we hear the sound of a key turning in a lock. Meanwhile, the door at back opens and LIESL enters, followed by CLARA, carrying two pillows.)

LIESL: I asked from you the room dirty-nine. Iss diss de room from Herr Vatelin? *(She puts her overnight bag on the table.)*

CLARA: I repeat, Madame, when guests are out, I can't let anyone into their room unless they've given me orders.

LIESL: *(Sitting near the table)* Aber donnerwetter! Venn I dell you he doldt me to vait for him *hier!* He vired me for chust dot! *Hier*, readt der delegram! …Iff you dond relief *me*, readt, you vill relief…

CLARA: Believe!

LIESL: *(Handing her a telegram)* Ach, you do relief? If you vish! *Hier* readt, you…

CLARA: *Ja, ja.*

LIESL: *Ach!* You sbeak Cherman?

CLARA: I can say "Ja", that's all. *(Reading.)* "Your husband knows everything, he found your letter in the wastepaper basket..." *(Stopping.)* Ah!

LIESL: *(Rising and taking back the telegram) Ach!* Dot iss *nicht* for you, dot's for me! *Nein,* readt *der* endt... *"Komm* to der Hotel Glimax."

CLARA: *(Taking the note and reading)* "Ask for my room and if I'm not there, wait for me. Vatelin."

LIESL: *(Recovering the telegram and pulling out of her bag a dressing-gown, night-cap, etc.) Also! Vell,* are you konfinced?

CLARA: Very well, Madame, you may wait here.

LIESL: *Sehr gut!*

CLARA: Be my guest!

LIESL: *(Fetching a lighted candle)* Vhere iss *das* toilet, *der* vatchroom?

CLARA: *(Opening the door at right)* In here, Madame.

LIESL: *(Carrying her dressing-gown and her nightcap into the room at right)* Ach! You vill pring me zum shteins off *bier.*

CLARA: Very good, Madame!

LIESL: *Danke,* Mamsel! *(She exits.)*

CLARA: *(Alone)* You don't have to ask where she's from! ...These Krauts can't go to the potty without their beer.

(VICTOR, showing in VATELIN:)

VICTOR: This is your room, Monsieur.

VATELIN: *(Overnight bag in hand)* Fine!

CLARA: *(To VICTOR)* You must be mistaken. This room is occupied, it's Monsieur Vatelin's room.

VATELIN: Well, *I'm* Monsieur Vatelin.

CLARA: But what about the two characters who were here just now?…

VATELIN: *(Going downstage and placing his bag behind the sofa)* Yes, yes, don't worry about it! They noted the error at the desk. They were the guests for room 59, but, through a mistake in the reservation, their telegram read number 39… They'll be informed when they get back.

CLARA: Very good, Monsieur!

VATELIN: *(To* VICTOR*)* Thank you, boy!…

*(*VATELIN, *just as* VICTOR *goes upstage to exit:)*

VATELIN: Ah! Listen, tell them downstairs that a lady will be asking for me, so give her the number of my room and show her up. *(He sits beside the table.)*

VICTOR: Very good, Monsieur! *(He runs out.)*

CLARA: Is Monsieur looking for a lady?

VATELIN: No thanks, I already have one.

CLARA: I wasn't offering one to Monsieur. It's just that a lady came asking for Monsieur a few minutes ago and now she's in there!

VATELIN: Already!

CLARA: Shall I inform her?

VATELIN: No, she's all right where she is, leave her there!

CLARA: Very good, Monsieur. I'll go get the beer. *(She exits at back.)*

VATELIN: *(Rising)* Yes, she's all right where she is! I'll see her soon enough! Oh, I'm in a foul mood! *(He sits at left. At that moment,* LIESL *is heard humming a Viennese waltz tune.)* There she is!…

LIESL: *(Entering at right)* Grispy! Dere you are!

VATELIN: *(Rising; drily)* At least an hour early!

LIESL: *Ach, nein!* I vass since ten minoots...

VATELIN: Ah!

LIESL: *Jawohl!* I vaited ofer dere! *Ach!* Grispy, how I am clad! ...But for vhy you shtand dere shtepping at me?

VATELIN: "Shtepping at you"?

LIESL: Like in "a flight of shteps."

VATELIN: What! "Flight of steps"! What do you mean, "flight of steps". A person doesn't say "steps", a person says "stairs". A flight of stairs. "Why are you staring at me?"

LIESL: *Ach!* Shteps, shtairs, shtairs, shteps, vot's der different? *Ach, mein* Grispy!

(LIESL throws her arms around his neck. VATELIN pulls his face back.)

LIESL: Voss! You don't vant I should giss you?

VATELIN: No!

LIESL: *Nein?*

VATELIN: *(Crossing right)* No. You wanted me to come, I came. It was my only means of avoiding a scandal in my home and keeping you from making a scene. I gave in, but I hope you've gotten it into your skull that all must be over between us.

LIESL: *Ach!* Grispy! Vhy you say dot? *Ach!* You bin *ein* naughty curl.

VATELIN: Naughty curl?

LIESL: *Ach!* Me who luffed you pecause you vos zo dender, zo shveet, so nize, in contest *von mein* husband, dot proot!

VATELIN: *(Aside)* Ah, so that was why you loved me, eh! Just you wait!

LIESL: You vos zo vell-mannered *mit der* ladies!

VATELIN: Me? Well, that's just where you're wrong!
Ah, you thought I was well-mannered, eh? Not in the
least. I'll show you how well-mannered I am. Ooh! la!
la! and damn it all! Darnation! And cootchy-cootchy-
coo! Ha! ha! ha! how's your old man? Shut your trap,
kiddo! What a kisser! Well, shove that up your pipe
and suck it! *(He sketches a cancan step, his left hand
striking the back of his neck, his right hand slapping the air
in front of his face.)* That's how well-mannered I am. *(He
sits beside the table.)*

LIESL: *(Crossing right and laughing) Ach*! How you vos
phoney dot vay!

VATELIN: Funny! Ah, so you think I'm funny, do
you! But you don't know me! I'm not nice, I'm not
sweet, I'm not tender! *(Rising)* That was all right in
Vienna, because I wasn't at home, but in France, I'm
headstrong, brutal, violent!

LIESL: You!

VATELIN: Absolutely, and I beat women, I do! *(In a gruff
voice)* Grrrrrrr!

LIESL: *(Almost collapsing with laughter) Ach*! Grispy!…

VATELIN: Don't take another step or I'll belt you one!

LIESL: *(As if taking up a challenge)* Vot did you zay?

VATELIN: *(More timidly)* I said, "Don't take another step
or I'll belt you one."

LIESL: You pelt? You?

VATELIN: That's right!

LIESL: *(Approaching him)* Chust you dry!

VATELIN: *(Pushing her away, the flat of his hand against her
upper arm)* There!

LIESL: *Ach!* You pelt! Zo! You vant pelt! *Also! Ein, zwei!* *(She takes up a boxing position.)* Go head, pelt! Eh? *(She punches him.) Und* zo! Eh? *Und* take dot! Eh? *Und* dot! Eh? *Und* dot! *Und* dot! *Und* dot!

VATELIN: *(Falling into a seat at left)* Oh dear! what's come over her?...

LIESL: Zo! He vants to pelt!

VATELIN: Enough! Oh my oh my oh my!

LIESL: Dirty Vrenchy! *(Embracing his neck from behind and kissing him) Ach!* I adore you!

(Knock at the door)

LIESL: *Herein! (She moves right.)*

VATELIN: *(Aside)* What a punch she's got!

CLARA: *(Entering with the beer)* Here's the beer!

LIESL: *(Watching* CLARA *enter with a tray with bottled beer and glasses) Ach! Gut!* Put it down dere, *danke!*

*(*CLARA *exits.)*

LIESL: *Also! (Uncorking the bottles.)* You got *eine kleine* vallopink!

*(*VATELIN *makes a face.)*

LIESL: You vant shtill to pelt your leedle Liesl?

VATELIN: Taking advantage of your womanhood!

LIESL: *(Going to him)* So you goink to pe nize to your leedle Liesl?

VATELIN: But, you birdbrain, won't anything stop you! Don't you realize that your husband knows the score?

LIESL: *Mein* huzbandt knows *der* shcore? He don't blay moosic!

VATELIN: It's an idiom! He knows everything, if you prefer! After all, if it hadn't been for my telegram...

LIESL: *Ach ja!* I vould haf mein huzbandt vollowink *mein* footshtairs.

VATELIN: No doubt about it! *(Changing his tone)* Except one doesn't say footstairs, one says footsteps. Feet don't have stairs, they have steps.

LIESL: Chust pefore venn I zaid "shteps", you dold me "shtairs".

VATELIN: No, excuse me, you said "flight of steps." Well, for flight, you say "stairs," but for other parts of the body, you say "steps." Merely an offhand observation… by the way. *(Taking up where he left off)* No, no! the part you want me to play is out of the question, I can't, I can't! If you won't be sensible, at least *I* will! Goodbye! *(He goes upstage.)*

LIESL: *(Catching him by the sleeve)* Grispy! Grispy! Shtay! Oh, shtay!

VATELIN: No, let go of me, let go!

LIESL: *Nein!*

VATELIN: No?

LIESL: All righdt, I vill gill meinzelf!

VATELIN: *(Placing his hat on the bed)* Again! For heaven's sake, this is blackmail! All right, gill yourself and leave me in peace! *(He comes downstage.)*

LIESL: *Sehr gut!* …I vill trink a glass *bier* und *denn* die! *(She pours herself a glass of beer.)*

VATELIN: Go ahead and die!

LIESL: *(Pouring beer)* Von't you haff a glass *bier*?

VATELIN: Huh?

LIESL: I zaid, Von't you haff a glass *bier*?

VATELIN: If you insist!

(LIESL pours VATELIN a glass of beer.)

LIESL: *(Pulling a vial of smelling salts from her pocket)* Von drop? Two drops?

VATELIN: I don't know, what's the usual, a spoonful?

LIESL: Ach, dot's a lot!

VATELIN: *(Holding out his glass)* Can't help it! I'm a greedy pig.

LIESL: Ach, neffer mindt! A shpoonful couldt gill a whole retchiment.

VATELIN: *(Casting aside his glass and rising)* Huh! What is it?

LIESL: Strychnine! *(She brings the vial to her lips.)*

VATELIN: *(Rushing to her to take the vial)* Wretched woman! Put it down!

LIESL: *Nein!* I vill trink it all *und denn* decrease pefore your fairy ice!

VATELIN: In Heaven's name! Liesl, I implore you!

LIESL: *(Trying to bring the vial to her lips)* Nein! *Leb wohl*, Grispy!

(In the struggle, LIESL and VATELIN do a few waltz steps.)

VATELIN: *(Preventing her)* Liesl, I'll give in, I'll do anything you ask! Anything you ask!

LIESL: Dot's vot you zay *now*!

VATELIN: No, no! Anything! Anything! I swear it.

LIESL: *Ja?*

VATELIN: Yes! ...*Ja!* ...*Ja!* ...Yes!

LIESL: *(Inhaling the smelling salts; aside)* Ah, dot's petter! *(She puts the vial in her pocket.)*

VATELIN: *(Aside)* All right, all right! If I've got to, let's get it over with! *(Aloud, hurrying along in order to speed things up.)* Yes, you're right! I've fought it long enough! Come on, Liesl, come on! I desire you, I want you.

Come on, come on! *(He has taken her in his arms and tries to drag her to the bed.)*

LIESL: *(Frightened, pulls away)* Ach! Nein, nein, Grispy, like dot I don't vant!

VATELIN: Then screw it! You know what you can do with it!

LIESL: *(Going to him)* All righdt, I vant, I vant!

VATELIN: If you're going to cool my ardor that way…

LIESL: *(Putting a hand over his mouth)* Ach, nein! Shoosh! Shoosh! Ve von't shtart on de wronk shtep!

VATELIN: What do you mean, "on the wrong step"? What an expression! You mean, on the wrong foot!

LIESL: *(Pushing him away)* Ach! Schrew it yourzelf! Like you zay! You're doink dis on burpose! Ven I zay shtairs, you zay shtep; ven I zay shtep, you zay foot. I don't know, it's nefer like I zay!

VATELIN: No, please, bawl me out!

LIESL: *(Immediately affectionate, putting her arms around his neck)* Nein, nein! I don't bawl oudt! It vos a choke! You luff me, I luff you!

VATELIN: We love one another!

LIESL: Vait! I go in dere! *(She goes a bit up right.)*

VATELIN: In there?

LIESL: Ja! You don't vant I should shtay in dis outvit.

VATELIN: Well, can't you change in here?

LIESL: *Hier? Ach!* In vront from you! *Himmel!*

VATELIN: Fine, fine, go on, go on.

(LIESL exits right.)

VATELIN: *(Going up to the bed)* Honestly, what a lesson! What a lesson! …I ought to go and jump off a bridge! Poor Vatelin, you've really got yourself into a mess this time! (*He sits on the edge of the bed, and loses himself in his thoughts. Under his weight, the bell on the audience-side of the bed starts ringing. After a long pause, and still in position:*) Curious how long the bells go on in this hotel?

(*At that moment, the door at left opens silently and* LUCIENNE *sticks her head out. She sees her husband's back and recognizes it, raises both arms to heaven and opens her mouth wide, but before she can cry out,* PONTAGNAC *has run to her, shaking his head "No", to indicate "Not yet". Meanwhile, his right hand has seized her right hand and he abruptly pushes her in front of him while his left hand rapidly closes the door behind him. This byplay must be absolutely mute and finish in the twinkling of an eye.*)

VATELIN: (*Rising and abruptly turning round*) Huh? (*Seeing no one and laughing*) Nothing! Well, this smells of mystery! Nobody moved in this room? And yet I heard something! (*Going to inspect the door at left.*) No, this is locked, the door's jammed. No, it must have been an illusion! All the same, there isn't any draft! It's that confounded Liesl… with her strychnine beer. (*Going to the wall-buzzer*) I'd better ring for someone to carry off her filthy suds. (*Reading the wall chart*) Chambermaid, two rings! Swell. (*He rings twice, then comes downstage.*) She may still get a hankering for it…

(*Someone knocks at the door.*)

VATELIN: Well, the chambermaid certainly doesn't dawdle. (*Aloud*) Come in!

SOLDIGNAC: (*Entering*) Goodbye!

VATELIN: (*Aside*) Soldignac! Sonuvabitch, her husband! (*Aloud*) Ah, it's you!

SOLDIGNAC: Ja! It's me!

VATELIN: Ha, ha, ha! Really! …What are you doing here?

SOLDIGNAC: *(Going to the table)* That intrigues you, does it?

VATELIN: I'll say!… *(Aside)* Good grief! And his wife's in the other room!

SOLDIGNAC: *(Sitting down)* I was downstairs at the desk when the bellhop you sent said: If anyone asks for Monsieur Vatelin, show him up to room 39.

VATELIN: *(Aside)* Ah! My bright idea of sending him with that message to the desk. *(He tries to move up near* LIESL.*)*

*(*SOLDIGNAC *rises and moving far left takes* VATELIN *by the arm.)*

(During this whole scene VATELIN *is very preoccupied and tries to reach the door at right.* SOLDIGNAC, *arm in arm with him, forces him to take a little stroll.)*

SOLDIGNAC: I came to this hotel for a rendezvous with someone who couldn't wait for me, and asked to be excused.

VATELIN: *(Whose mind is elsewhere)* Yes, yes, yes.

SOLDIGNAC: She had to look after her sick old mother. *(Stopping and looking at him.)* Am I boring you? *(He drops his arm.)*

VATELIN: *(As if in a dream)* Not at all! I'm with you! You were saying, "Mother". I'm delighted! …You're a mother!

SOLDIGNAC: Who?

VATELIN: You!

SOLDIGNAC: *Nein*, not me…her!…

VATELIN: Ah! her!

SOLDIGNAC: *Ja!* …Her sick old mother.

VATELIN: Ah, her mother! …So the old lady's sick, is she?

SOLDIGNAC: So what could I do? …Well, I suppose you'd say why not leave…

VATELIN: *(Shoving him to the door)* Leave? Why not? Go on! Get out! Don't hang around for my sake.

SOLDIGNAC: *(Coming down left) Ach! Nein, nein!* …it was a for-instance! *(He places his cane near the fireplace.)*

VATELIN: Ah, it was a for-instance. *(Aside)* What a shame. *(Aloud)* No, I suggested it because I know that you're usually in a hurry.

SOLDIGNAC: *Ach ja!* In the daytime, but at night I always have time! *(He stretches out on the sofa.)*

VATELIN: *(Aside)* Well, this is going to be jolly!

SOLDIGNAC: *Nein!* Leave—I just couldn't. Since I knew I'd be at this hotel tonight, I made a date to meet the police inspector here.

VATELIN: *(Falling on to the chair next to the table)* The police inspector!

SOLDIGNAC: Of course! …You know that I intend to nab my wife tonight.

VATELIN: *(Aside)* Good Lord! What if he suspects me? *(Aloud)* She isn't here! She isn't here!

SOLDIGNAC: Who? My wife? I know that. She's at Rue Rockypain.

VATELIN: *(Rising)* Oh, yes, yes! *(Aside)* He knows nothing.

SOLDIGNAC: The Inspector must be in the act of surprising her at this very moment.

VATELIN: *(Goes up to the door at right)* Yes, yes, yes, yes.

SOLDIGNAC: *(Rising)* And to be absolutely certain, he's had her trailed since this morning. Am I boring you?

VATELIN: *(Going to him)* No! no! no! …You were saying: "Mother… her old mother is sick."

SOLDIGNAC: *Ach, nein*! Not any more.

VATELIN: Ah! she died! …That's always the next step!

SOLDIGNAC: *Aber nein*! …I was saying, "My wife…"

VATELIN: Ah yes, your wife…who's over there…

SOLDIGNAC: What?

VATELIN: Who's over there…Rue Rockypain!…

SOLDIGNAC: *Ja!* …He had her trailed!…

VATELIN: *(More and more nervous)* She went for a hike! …Along a trail!… *(He goes back upstage.)*

SOLDIGNAC: The Inspector should be sending me a report as soon as it's over.

VATELIN: *(At back right)* Perfect, perfect!

SOLDIGNAC: But what's the matter with you, you're acting so nervous?

VATELIN: *(Going up to* SOLDIGNAC*)* Me! Nervous! Not at all! Do I seem nervous?

SOLDIGNAC: Yes, are you ill?

VATELIN: *(Thumbs in his waistcoat pockets)* No, yes, oh! a bit, very slightly!

SOLDIGNAC: Indigestion?

VATELIN: *(Distracted)* Eh?

SOLDIGNAC: He doesn't hear a word! *(Rubbing his belly)* Indigestion!

VATELIN: Huh? No, yes! You know, somewhere in between!

SOLDIGNAC: "Somewhere in between"! Well, that's normal.

VATELIN: Quite so! That's it! I'm a bit normal! Nothing to worry about.

(VATELIN, *going upstage while* SOLDIGNAC *sits on the sofa:*)

VATELIN: Good Lord! Good Lord!

(*At that moment, the door at right half opens and* LIESL's *arm drops her blouse on to the chair next to the door.*)

SOLDIGNAC: (*Who saw the arm*) Ach! Pretty! Very pretty!

VATELIN: (*Who has turned on hearing* SOLDIGNAC, *aside*) Holy Moses! Liesl's arm!... (*Aloud*) You saw that? ... It's... it's an arm.

SOLDIGNAC: (*Seated on the sofa*) Ach! So I see! Very pretty, ah, you dirty dog! Whose arm is it? (*He puts his hat on the table.*)

VATELIN: I don't know! It's not from around here! It's a strange arm...it must have just arrived! ...It arrived, but it didn't exactly arrive...it's an arm from next door!

SOLDIGNAC: Wise guy! ...It's your wife's arm.

VATELIN: That's it! You said it, it's your wife's arm... uh, *my* wife's arm...my wife from next door!...

(*He picks up the blouse, but just as he's about to go upstage, the arm reappears holding* LIESL's *skirt.* VATELIN *rushes to it, snatches the dress and tosses it and the blouse under the bed.*)

SOLDIGNAC: Well, my dear fellow...but where did you go?

VATELIN: (*Coming back downstage*) Here! Here I am!

SOLDIGNAC: Sit down here next to me!

VATELIN: (*Sitting on the back of the sofa, aside*) Now he's moving in!

SOLDIGNAC: My compliments, Madame has quite an arm!

(*At that moment,* LIESL, *unaware of her husband's presence, walks boldly on stage. She is in a dressing-gown and*

nightcap with ear-flaps. Recognizing her husband, she
utters a stifled scream and rushes back into the washroom.
SOLDIGNAC, *hearing the scream, turns his head, but*
VATELIN, *forestalling his intention, seizes his head in both*
hands and turns it toward his own face.)

SOLDIGNAC: *Ach! Was ist los?*

VATELIN: I beg your pardon…it was my wife, she was
in a state of undress, so…

SOLDIGNAC: Ah, sorry. *Ach!* You did the right thing.

VATELIN: I'll say I did! Well, come and play a round of
billiards. *(He takes him by the arm and drags him off.)*

SOLDIGNAC: *Jawohl!* That I will! Happy to!… *(He takes
his hat.)*

VATELIN: *(Aside)* It's the only way to get rid of him.

SOLDIGNAC: We would embarrass the lady if we stayed
here.

VATELIN: You're too modest! Speak for yourself.

SOLDIGNAC: *Ach!*

VATELIN: *(Aside)* I'll score five combination shots and
come right back. *(Aloud)* Let's go!

SOLDIGNAC: Let's go.

(A knock at the door)

VATELIN: What is it now?

SOLDIGNAC: Come in!

VATELIN: *(Aside)* Well, he's got a nerve!… *(He comes a
bit downstage right.)*

RÉDILLON: *(Enters, holding the bag he took away with him)*
I beg your pardon, gentlemen!

VATELIN: Oh no! Rédillon!

RÉDILLON: I must have mistaken my overnight bag just now. *(Recognizing* VATELIN*)* Vatelin! What, you here? *(He puts the bag on the chair beside the table.)*

VATELIN: Uh, yes! It is me. I missed the train... I'll explain the whole thing to you. Come and play a round of billiards with this gentleman. *(He pushes him towards* SOLDIGNAC.*)*

RÉDILLON: This gentleman? ...But I don't know him.

VATELIN: Monsieur...Soldignac, Monsieur Rédillon. Come play a round of billiards!

RÉDILLON: *(Trying to get out of it)* Me? But I don't know how to play.

VATELIN: Never mind! *He* knows, he'll teach you.

RÉDILLON: *(Moving right)* Certainly not! Anyway, I haven't the time! I'm expected! *(He sits on the sofa.)*

VATELIN: *(Forcing him to rise)* Really? Well then, don't sit down! ...Hardly worth it, we're on our way downstairs. *(He drags him along.)*

RÉDILLON: Well, in that case! ...Picture this...

VATELIN: No, no, we haven't got the time, you can tell us about later on. Where's my hat? *(He goes to the bed.)*

RÉDILLON: What's wrong with him? He's making me sweat, I must say! *(He goes to drink the glass of beer nearby.)*

VATELIN: *(Wearing his hat)* There it is, come along! *(Pulling the glass away)* No, don't drink it, we haven't got the time!

(A knock on the door at back.)

SOLDIGNAC: *(Lighting a cigarette at the fireplace)* Come in!

VATELIN: Again! He's driving me crazy with his "Come in"s!

CLARA: *(Entering)* Did Monsieur ring?

VATELIN: Yes I did, at least half an hour ago. Take away these glasses and things.

(He pulls away the glass that RÉDILLON *is bringing to his lips, and hands it to* CLARA.*)*

CLARA: Very good, Monsieur. *(She carries off the tray of bottles and glasses.)*

VATELIN: *(Pushing* RÉDILLON *ahead of him)* And now, let's skedaddle!

RÉDILLON: But my bag! I came to get my bag!

VATELIN: *(Handing* RÉDILLON *the bag he had just brought back)* Well, take your bag and go!

RÉDILLON: No, I don't want this one! …I just brought it back!

VATELIN: *(Handing him* LIESL's *bag)* Well, is this the one?

RÉDILLON: *(Taking the bag)* I don't know! Isn't it yours?

VATELIN: No! *(He puts* PINCHARD's *bag on the table in place of* LIESL's.*)*

RÉDILLON: Then this one must be hers. Let's go! *(He goes upstage.)*

SOLDIGNAC: *(Going upstage at the same time)* Let's go!

VATELIN: All right! Go on ahead. I'll leave a message and join you.

*(*RÉDILLON *and* SOLDIGNAC *exit at back.)*

VATELIN: *(Who has gone to the door right)* Quick! Liesl!

LIESL: *(Entering)* I couldt *komm* in? Dey iss gone?

VATELIN: Yes! In a manner of speaking. But they're waiting for me downstairs! I'm obliged to go and play a round of billiards with your husband! For pity's sake, while I'm away a little while, don't stir from this room. I'm going to lock you in and take away the key for safety's sake. Now if anyone comes, hide in that washroom and don't leave it until I've come back for you… Understand?

LIESL: *Gewiss!*

SOLDIGNAC: *(Off)* Vatelin! Vatelin!

VATELIN: *(Quickly)* It's him! Hide!

(LIESL barely has time to hide by pressing herself against the bed.)

SOLDIGNAC: *(In the doorway)* Look here, Vatelin!

VATELIN: All right ! I'm coming, I'm coming! *(He exits, taking care to remove the key and double-lock the door behind him.)*

LIESL: *(Alone, coming downstage)* Ach! How I vass afraidt! *Ach! Lieber Gott,* venn I zee dere *mein* huzbandt, all *mein* couratch runs avay! *Ach, nein, nein!* I don't vant no more, I vant to go avay… *(Looking for her clothes on the chair where she thought she placed them.)* My closes! … Vhere did he poot *mein* closes?…

(People talking in the corridor)

LIESL: *Ach, mein Gott,* vot it iss now?… *(She rushes into the room at right.)*

PINCHARD: *(Off)* Oh great! The key isn't in the lock and I forgot to ask for one downstairs! *(Calling)* Boy! Will you please open this for me?

VICTOR: *(Off)* Very good, Monsieur.

(The key turns in the lock. The door opens and PINCHARD and MME PINCHARD enter. VICTOR stands aside to let them in.)

PINCHARD: Thank you, lad.

VICTOR: Don't mention it, Monsieur. *(He exits, closing the door behind him.)*

PINCHARD: *(To his wife whom he supports and leads forward)* There, there! Stop moaning! It'll pass! Come,

sit down here! *(He helps her to sit.)* Confounded
gas attacks! You had to have a relapse during the
performance. We had to leave before it was over.
(Noticing his bag) Ah, they brought up my bag! I knew I
must have left it downstairs.

*(*PINCHARD, *to* MME PINCHARD, *who watches him with a
meek and suffering look. These and the following lines are
spoken by the lips only:)*

PINCHARD: Well, feel any better?

*(*MME PINCHARD *shakes her head "No".)*

PINCHARD: *(Soundlessly)* You're still feeling ill?

*(*MME PINCHARD *nods her head "Yes".)*

PINCHARD: Stick out your tongue.

*(*MME PINCHARD *does so.)*

PINCHARD: It looks all right!

*(*MME PINCHARD *makes a face, signifying "It can't".)*

PINCHARD: You know, you ought to go to bed.

(Gesture of MME PINCHARD: *"You think so? Maybe you're
right.")*

PINCHARD: Of course I'm right!

*(*MME PINCHARD, *with a rueful smile, goes "Good night"
with her head.)*

PINCHARD: Good night!

*(*MME PINCHARD *goes upstage a bit, then returns to
PINCHARD and kisses him.)*

PINCHARD: *(Aloud)* Ah, yes! Our anniversary! *(He kisses
her on the forehead.)* Twenty-five years!

*(*MME PINCHARD *goes, with mournful step, between the
wall and the bed, to undress.)*

PINCHARD: *(Aloud)* I'll prepare her a sedative. *(He goes
to the fireplace, takes the lighted candle and comes back to*

the table. He puts the light down on the table and begins to rummage in his bag.) Where is my first-aid kit? *(Pulling out his slippers.)* My slippers! *(He throws them down in front of him, then pulls out another pair.)* Ah! hers. Look, Bunnykins! ...Slippers! ...The fuzzy ones! *(He brings them to his wife.)*

MME PINCHARD: *(Behind the bed)* Thanks!

PINCHARD: *(Pulling a night-gown out of the bag)* And a nightie! *(To his wife)* Bunnykins! Nightie!

(PINCHARD hands MME PINCHARD the night-gown.)

MME PINCHARD: Thanks. *(She puts it on.)*

PINCHARD: *(Back in the bag)* Ah, here's my first-aid kit. *(Opening it)* Laudanum! Laudanum! Here's the laudanum.

MME PINCHARD: *(From behind the bed)* My wide-tooth comb, hand me my wide-tooth comb.

PINCHARD: *(Pulling it out of the bag)* The wide-tooth comb! Here! *(He hands it to her across the bed; then, taking the glass, the carafe and the spoon from the night table at the foot of the bed)* Now, let's mix a dose!

(PINCHARD comes downstage to the table and prepares the mixture. MME PINCHARD, minus her blouse, her hair down to her shoulders, sits on the bed to comb her hair. The buzzer, placed under the mattress on her side, naturally starts ringing non-stop. He pays no attention to it; he sits at the table.)

PINCHARD: *(Counting drops)* One, two, three... Ah! who's the bastard playing around with bells at this time of the night? ...Four, five, six, there, six drops! *(He places the glass on the table and gets up.)* Oh, he's starting to get on my nerves with his ringing! *(Running and opening the door at back, and shouting into the corridor.)* Hey, Quasimodo, when are you going to stop ringing your bells?

VOICE: *(In the corridor)* Hey, who's ringing like that?

PINCHARD: *(Answering it)* I don't know, Monsieur, it's insufferable. *(Shouting)* that's enough! There are people trying to sleep!

MME PINCHARD: *(Rising to look out; the ringing stops)* What on earth is the matter?

PINCHARD: *(Now that the ringing is over)* Ah, it's stopped, and none too soon!

VOICE: About time too! Good night, Monsieur.

PINCHARD: Sweet dreams, Monsieur. *(He closes the door at back.)*

MME PINCHARD: What was it, Pinchard?

PINCHARD: Nothing, nothing. *(Pushing her back to bed)* Go on, lie down, it's late, I'll join you. I made that swine hold his noise! *(He takes off his tunic.)*

(Meanwhile, MME PINCHARD lies down. The ringing starts all over again.)

PINCHARD: Oh great! Now they're starting all over again! This is getting to be a bore! *(As he leans on the bed in order to remove his shoes and put on his slippers, the buzzer on his side starts ringing in time with the other one.)* What, now there's somebody else who's decided to join the band! ...Impossible, there can't be a bell-ringing contest going on in this hotel! ...Whoever heard of such a racket!... *(He begins to remove his shoes and turns his back to the door at left.)*

(LUCIENNE, zooming in, followed by PONTAGNAC:)

LUCIENNE: Now I've got you, you wretch!

(LUCIENNE closes in on PINCHARD and grabs him by the shoulders. He loses his balance and falls seated on the ground. His back is still to the other characters and he has removed only one shoe.)

LUCIENNE & PONTIGNAC: It's not him! *(They rush back into the room at left.)*

PINCHARD: *(Gets up, shoe in hand, and, seeing no one, limps around peering into corners)* Where did they go? Where did they get to?

VICTOR: *(Rapidly entering at the back)* What's the matter, Monsieur, what's the matter?

PINCHARD: *(Putting on a slipper)* Huh?

CLARA: *(Entering like* VICTOR*)* Is Monsieur ringing like that?

PINCHARD: Me?

MANAGER: *(Entering like* VICTOR *and* CLARA*)* Really, Monsieur! You mustn't ring like that! Do you want to wake up the whole hotel?

PINCHARD: What? Am I the one ringing those bells?

HOTEL GUEST: *(Entering in dressing-gown and night-cap)* It's high time you stopped ringing, Monsieur! ...My wife can't get a wink of sleep!

SECOND HOTEL GUEST: *(Entering)* Who's ringing all those bells?

HOTEL GUESTS: *(A succession, male and female, in various states of dress and undress, clamor of exclamations:)* What's the matter? Why are they ringing? When is this racket going to stop? *(Etc, etc)*

PINCHARD: Hey! Who are all these people? When are you going to get out?

MANAGER: As soon as you stop ringing.

ALL: Yes, yes!

PINCHARD: How am I ringing? Where do you see me ringing? Who do you see ringing? Is anyone here ringing?

MANAGER: After all, Monsieur!...

PINCHARD: How dare you break in on people in this way? Go on, get the hell out of here!

ALL: *(Howling him down)* Oh!

PINCHARD: *(Furious, next to the bed)* Get the bloody hell out!

(To give more force to his command, PINCHARD *stresses each syllable by banging his fist on the mattress; the buzzer responds with a curt ringing: "Ding, ding, ding!"* PINCHARD *stops, astonished stares at the mattress, and coolly punches it three times in a row. The buzzer, consequently, responds with three fresh and distinct "Ding! Ding! Ding!s".)*

PINCHARD: Aha! The bed is what's ringing!

ALL: The bed!

PINCHARD: Definitely! *(He pulls out the buzzer from his side of the mattress.)* Well, well! that's a fine gag! ...I'd like to get my hands on the practical joker who gets his kicks playing pranks like this!'

ALL: *(Astonished)* Ah!

PINCHARD: Listen! It's still going on! I'll bet there's another one under the...under my wife!

(They all turn towards the back. The MANAGER *and the* HOTEL GUESTS *push in between the bed and the wall, trying to pull out the other buzzer.)*

MME PINCHARD: *(Who has understood nothing of all this)* What's going on? What do you want from me? My love! Pinchard! There are men after me!

PINCHARD: They're not after *you*!

MANAGER: Fear not, Madame. *(Finding the buzzer)* Ah yes, here's the other one!

PINCHARD: *(Taking the buzzer and coming downstage)*
There! What did I tell you? Ah, I'd love to know what
all this is supposed to mean!

MANAGER: But, Monsieur, I haven't the foggiest notion!

PINCHARD: If this is the way unsuspecting travelers
are imposed on for fun in your hotel, I'll lodge a
complaint, you know!

MANAGER: Oh, Monsieur, I assure you…

PINCHARD: *(Handing the buzzers to the* MANAGER*)* All
right, all right! Get out of here, all of you! And leave us
alone.

*(Everyone leaves; he brutally slams the door on the last to
go.)*

PINCHARD: A regular barracks room brawl! *(He reaches
right.)*

MME PINCHARD: *(On her knees in bed, clutching a pillow
to her bosom)* But what's going on?

PINCHARD: *(Sitting beside the table)* She didn't hear a
thing! Well, Bunnykins, you were lucky.

MME PINCHARD: What did all those people want?

PINCHARD: *(Shaking his head)* Nothing! Nothing! *(He
pulls off the other shoe.)*

MME PINCHARD: Oh, I was so frightened! My pains
were just beginning to calm down, and now they're
back worse than ever. *(She lies down.)*

PINCHARD: *(Rising)* Oh, the swine! Listen, you ought to
put a mustard plaster on it. *(He puts on the other slipper.)*

MME PINCHARD: What?

PINCHARD: *(Lips only)* Why don't you put on a mustard
plaster?

MME PINCHARD: How am I supposed to understand? Don't talk in the shadows! I can't see what you're saying!

PINCHARD: *(Taking the candle and lighting up his face; lips only)* You ought to put a mustard plaster on it.

MME PINCHARD: You're right there! With a few drops of laudanum, it should do me all the good in the world. But where can we get one?

PINCHARD: *(Displaying his bag, lips only)* I have what's needed in here! I only have to make it up! Wait! *(He rings, then opening the bag, pulls out a packet of powdered mustard. Aside)* When we left and I saw she was under the weather, I laid in a supply just in case! There was a little corner of the bag empty, she wanted to stick ham sandwiches in it... I preferred to fill it with the makings of a mustard plaster! I see I did the right thing!

VICTOR: *(Entering at the back)* Did Monsieur ring?

PINCHARD: *(Throwing the bag behind the night table)* Yes, it was me this time. I want to make a mustard plaster... for Bunnykins...I mean, for Madame, who is in pain.

VICTOR: But, Monsieur, there's nobody in the kitchen at this hour.

PINCHARD: Of course not! A moment ago this room was packed with people, and now there's nobody in the kitchen! At least you've got a gas stove?

VICTOR: Oh yes! there's a stove, Monsieur!

(PINCHARD, putting his tunic back on, helped by VICTOR:)

PINCHARD: All right, you can show me the way, and I'll make it myself.

VICTOR: Very good, Monsieur! Will you allow me, Major?

PINCHARD: *(Handing him the tunic)* No, I will not allow you! I order you to! *(Byplay.)* If I ever run into you in sick bay, I'll slap such a plaster on you! *(Candle in hand and lips only, to his wife.)* I'm going downstairs to make the mustard plaster. I'll be back in five minutes. Try to sleep in the meantime.

MME PINCHARD: Try to sleep! ...Don't worry! ...If I can! ...Don't be long!

PINCHARD: No!

(MME PINCHARD turns towards the wall. PINCHARD and VICTOR exit. The stage is empty for a moment. LIESL comes cautiously out of the washroom.)

LIESL: *Der* noise it vos ofer! But vass iss goink on aroundt *hier*? *Und* Vatelin nefer came back. *Ach nein*! I vill get tressed *und denn* I go... But vhere did he trow *mein* closes? *(She looks everywhere ends up at the bed, and notices MME PINCHARD's back.) Gott in Himmel!* Dere iss somevun in der bedt! *(Panic-stricken, she rushes back into the washroom.)*

(Once again the stage remains empty. Suddenly we hear a key turning in the lock of the door at back, and then a push against the door, which resists.)

VATELIN: *(Off)* Hey, what's the matter with this lock?

(New sound of a key and a push from VATELIN, the door opens.)

VATELIN: *(Entering)* Stupid of me! I was turning it the wrong way. Instead of opening it, I was double-locking it. *(He closes the door.)* Oh my, oh my, that Soldignac sticks like glue! ...I thought I'd never shake him off! ...Let's go and set Liesl free.

(Snoring from the bed)

VATELIN: Huh! Someone snoring in here! *(Pulling the bed-curtain aside.)* What, she went to bed? No, she's unbelievable! Nothing fazes her!... *(Taking his bag from behind the sofa, he places it on the table and pulls out a pair*

*of slippers which he throws in front of the bed; then he sets
up a chair near the bed, beside the night table. On it he will
place all his clothing.)* Ah! talk about Teutonic phlegm!
…My word, since she's asleep, why wake her? There's
that much gained. I'll lie down nice and quiet… taking
good care not to arouse her from her restful slumber…
(Starting to undress.) Restful for me! Let sleeping dogs
lie. *(Coming downstage, he stumbles over the shoes left
by* PINCHARD, *picks them up.)* No, would you believe
the feet these Germanic women have! *(He has pulled
off his own shoes and goes to deposit them outside with
PINCHARD's.)* Man! but I'm thirsty! *(Sees the tumbler left
on the table by* PINCHARD.*)* I'm in luck! Very thoughtful
of you, Madame Soldignac. *(He drinks.)* Ah! that's an
improvement… *(He finishes undressing.)* My eyelids
are heavy…I don't think it'll take long to fall asleep…
Come on, let's go to bed and quietly, lest we awaken
my mistress. *(He slips into bed.)* Good grief, she takes up
room…I don't dare shove her over, it would wake her
up. Look, I forgot my hat. *(He throws it on the foot of the
bed.)* It'll keep my feet warm. Snug as bugs in a rug…
Man! I'm sleepy…I don't know, I think I've got sleepier
since I had a drink from that glass… What did she put
in it? …Strychnine, like before! Strychnine… *(He falls
asleep.)*

(The door opens and VICTOR *lets in* PINCHARD *and his
mustard plaster. Then* VICTOR *puts the candle on the
mantelpiece.)*

PINCHARD: Thanks!

*(*VICTOR *exits.* PINCHARD *blows on the mustard plaster
which he moistens with laudanum.)*

PINCHARD: *(To his wife as he starts towards the bed)* Here
you are, Bunnykins, watch out, it's hot! *(He uncovers
VATELIN with his right hand and with his left hand applies
the mustard plaster to his stomach.)*

VATELIN: *(Howling)* Aaaagh!

PINCHARD: What's the matter?

VATELIN: Who goes there? Stop, thief!

PINCHARD: A man in my wife's bed!

MME PINCHARD: *(Waking up)* Who's there? ...Ah, my stars, a man in my bed!...

VATELIN: Who on earth is this woman?

PINCHARD: *(Flying at his throat)* You cad! What are you doing here?

VATELIN: *(Getting out of the bed)* Will you let go of me!

ALL THREE: Help! Help!

PINCHARD: *(Shouting)* There's a man in my wife's bed!

VATELIN: Will you let go of me!

(LUCIENNE, surging in followed by PONTAGNAC:)

LUCIENNE: Now I've got you, you wretch!

VATELIN: Heavens, my wife!

(He pushes PINCHARD away, picks up his clothes on the run and scampers off, carrying the chair with him.)

PINCHARD: *(To LUCIENNE)* You are a witness, he was in Bunnykin's bed, Madame.

LUCIENNE: I saw it clearly, Monsieur!

PINCHARD: *(Running in hot pursuit)* Catch him! He was in Bunnykin's bed! ...My wife's bed!

MME PINCHARD: *(Who, during the preceding, has arisen and taken her slippers and skirt)* My husband! Pinchard! Where are you going? *(She rushes out in hot pursuit.)*

PONTAGNAC: *(To LUCIENNE)* Well, are you convinced?

LUCIENNE: Oh yes, the traitor!

PONTAGNAC: Was I right in telling you to stay, you who were so ready to go home?

LUCIENNE: Yes, you were right! Thank God, I've made up my mind now.

PONTAGNAC: I certainly hope you intend to take revenge!

LUCIENNE: Yes, I swear it to you!

PONTAGNAC: You know what you promised: "If ever I have proof of my husband's infidelity, I'll give him tit for tat on the spot!"

LUCIENNE: And I won't go back on my word! Ah, I'll show you that I'm a woman who means what she says!

PONTAGNAC: Bravo!

LUCIENNE: I said I would take a lover. Well, I do take that lover!

PONTAGNAC: Ah! I'm the happiest of mortals!

LUCIENNE: And if my husband asks you who my lover is, you can tell him!

PONTAGNAC: Oh, it's hardly worth the trouble.

LUCIENNE: It's his own best friend! ...Ernest Rédillon!

PONTAGNAC: *(Choking)* Huh! Réd...!

LUCIENNE: Farewell, I go to take revenge. *(She exits quickly out left.)*

PONTAGNAC: *(Running after her)* Lucienne! For heaven's sake! Lucienne! *(He rushes to the door which he finds locked.)* Locked!...

(PONTAGNAC *runs to the back and bumps into the* FIRST POLICE INSPECTOR, *followed by two* POLICEMEN *and* SOLDIGNAC.)

FIRST POLICE INSPECTOR: Stop!... In the name of the law!...

PONTAGNAC: Inspector!

SOLDIGNAC: *(A billiard cue in hand)* Ah, there he is, her "Liebster"! *(He places his billiard cue near the fireplace, takes off his coat, and starts shadow-boxing.)*

FIRST POLICE INSPECTOR: *(To* PONTAGNAC*)* We know it all, Monsieur! You are here with this gentleman's wife!

PONTAGNAC: Me!

FIRST POLICE INSPECTOR: Where is your accomplice hiding?

PONTAGNAC: My accomplice!

FIRST POLICE INSPECTOR: *(To a* POLICEMAN*)* Search the premises, officer!

PONTAGNAC: *(Aside)* What is he saying?

*(*POLICEMAN, *who has gone into the room at right, returns dragging* LIESL*:)*

POLICEMAN: Madame!...

PONTAGNAC: What is all this?

LIESL: *(Seeing* SOLDIGNAC*)* Mein huzbandt!

SOLDIGNAC: *(Turning around)* My wife!

*(*LIESL *and* SOLDIGNAC *argue in German.)*

SECOND POLICE INSPECTOR: *(Entering through the door at left, followed by* CLOTILDE*)* In the name of the law!

PONTAGNAC: Another one! *(Recognizing his wife.)* My wife!

CLOTILDE: *(To the* SECOND POLICE INSPECTOR*)* Do your duty, Inspector! *(She rapidly exits out left.)*

PONTAGNAC: *(Running to her)* Clotilde!...

SOLDIGNAC: *(Stopping him on the way)* Now it's just the two of us!

(He punches him while, for her part, LIESL *punches the* POLICEMAN *who won't let her go.)*

RÉDILLON: *(Entering at back. He is holding* LIESL*'s bag)*
Well, what's going on in here?

*(*RÉDILLON, *seeing the* INSPECTORs *stare at him:)*

RÉDILLON: I beg your pardon, I took the wrong bag!

*(*RÉDILLON *quickly exchanges bags with* VATELIN*'s which is on the table and runs out back while the punching continues. Tableau)*

(Curtain)

END OF ACT TWO

ACT THREE

(RÉDILLON's *den.* GÉRÔME *enters at the back. He holds, folded under his left arm,* RÉDILLON's *clothes and* ARMANDINE's *skirt, and both pairs of shoes, which he has just polished.)*

GÉRÔME: Another skirt! Always skirts! ...He's incorrigible! But what can you do about it, I ask myself. There you have it, the youth of today, burning the candle at both ends! Skirt-chasing! ...Everybody's chasing skirts. I'm the only one not chasing skirts! And that what's called being "up to date"! *(He knocks at the door up right.)*

RÉDILLON: *(Off)* What is it?

GÉRÔME: It's me, Gérôme.

RÉDILLON: *(Sticking his head out)* Well, what?

GÉRÔME: It's eleven o'clock!

RÉDILLON: Fine! It's eleven o'clock!... *(He slams the door in his face.)*

GÉRÔME: *(Getting it on the nose)* Yes! *(Aside)* And there you have it! Bang! A door in your face! And I was there when he was born! No respect nowadays! ... And his father was my foster-brother, who made me promise on his deathbed to keep an eye on him! ... But, my poor Marcellin, how do you expect me to keep an eye on your son! Do I have any control over him? Does he even listen to me?... It's as if I told the Prince of Monaco to keep an eye on Africa... When I mention morality, he calls me an old nincompoop, and when all's said and done, I'm still the one that's got to clean up after the floozies he brings home!

(We hear talking in RÉDILLON's *room and the door opens.)*

GÉRÔME: Ah! they finally decided to get up! *(He exits through the door down right, carrying off the clothes and shoes.)*

*(*ARMANDINE *enters, followed by* RÉDILLON. *She drags herself forward. Her hair is simply bound at the neck, and she is wrapped up in a man's dressing-gown. On entering, she catches her feet in it and almost falls.)*

ARMANDINE: Your dressing-gown's too long. *(She goes to the fireplace.)*

RÉDILLON: *(Dropping on to the divan)* It's too long for you, not for me!

ARMANDINE: *(Arranging her hair)* I wasn't talking about you, since I'm the one wearing it! ...Then too, what was the big idea of bringing me every overnight bag in the hotel except my own, one after another?

RÉDILLON: How was I to know which one was yours?

ARMANDINE: Anyway, in that crowd you might have had the luck to come across it. *(She leaves the fireplace.)*

RÉDILLON: *(Yawning)* Oh well!...

ARMANDINE: *(Looking at him)* Well, what next, buddy boy!

RÉDILLON: What?

ARMANDINE: Everything all right?

RÉDILLON: Oh yes! ...I'm just worn out, that's all!

ARMANDINE: *(Sitting near the table)* After eleven hours in bed!

(GÉRÔME *appears holding a feather duster. He stops and looks at* RÉDILLON *in pity.*)

RÉDILLON: But only six hours of sleep. *(He yawns.)*

GÉRÔME: *(Starting out the door up right)* The very idea of getting into such a state!

RÉDILLON: What do you want, Gérôme?

GÉRÔME: *(Sulking)* Nothing!

RÉDILLON: Then why are you glaring at me?

GÉRÔME: Ernest, you're burning yourself out, my boy!

ARMANDINE: Eh?

RÉDILLON: What?

GÉRÔME: You hurt me!

RÉDILLON: Will you leave me the hell in peace! Did anybody ask you anything?

GÉRÔME: I don't need you to ask me, I can say it! You hurt me! *(He exits at the back.)*

RÉDILLON: Glad to do it! Did you ever hear of such a thing! *(On the divan.)* I'm sorry, he's an old family retainer.

ARMANDINE: *(In the armchair)* He is a bit familiar!

RÉDILLON: Well, yes! because he's one of the family! He's my foster-uncle!

ARMANDINE: Your foster-uncle?

RÉDILLON: In other words, his mother was my father's wet nurse. We're milk relations.

ARMANDINE: All the same, it sounds funny to hear him talk to you so chummily, and you have to put up with it.

RÉDILLON: What can you do, he saw me being born. I didn't. *(Yawning)* Lord, am I tired. *(He stretches out on the divan, head towards the audience.)*

ARMANDINE: *(Rising)* Ah, poor Ernest! It's not as if you broke the record! *(She goes to him.)*

RÉDILLON: I never claimed to be the champion of France.

ARMANDINE: *(One knee on the divan between* RÉDILLON's *legs)* You do all right. *(She kisses him.)* Somebody'd think my kissing bores you!

RÉDILLON: *(Without conviction)* No!

ARMANDINE: *(Seated)* So! Already!

RÉDILLON: Certainly not! But, after all, come on!... *(Imploring)* Give it a rest!

ARMANDINE: Just like a man! They're only loving the night before. *(She rises.)*

RÉDILLON: Or the day after the day after!

ARMANDINE: Oo! Doll-baby! *(She kisses him.)*

GÉRÔME: *(Appears at back, carrying a full wineglass on a tray; to* ARMANDINE, *while stepping between them)* I beg of you, Madame, show mercy.

ARMANDINE: *(Crossing left, aside)* Well, what's eating him?

GÉRÔME: *(Staring at* RÉDILLON*)* Just look at that face?

RÉDILLON: I'm going to throw you out, hear me?

GÉRÔME: I don't care, I won't go! Here, drink this!

RÉDILLON: No.

GÉRÔME: Drink it!

RÉDILLON: *(Foul-tempered)* I need the patience of a saint! *(He takes the glass.)*

ARMANDINE: What is that stuff?

GÉRÔME: It's coca.

ARMANDINE: What?

GÉRÔME: *(Going to her)* Coca wine! It's a pick-me-up! *(In an undertone to* ARMANDINE*)* For pity's sake, Madame, remember he's only a baby, he's only thirty-two. He's not like me!…

RÉDILLON: *(Sitting on the divan, drinking)* What are you whispering to the lady?

GÉRÔME: Nothing, nothing, nothing.

ARMANDINE: *(Mocking)* Yes, we have secrets of our own.

GÉRÔME: There! It's none of your business!

RÉDILLON: I beg your pardon. *(He hands the glass to* GÉRÔME.*)* Anybody come to call?

GÉRÔME: *(Scornfully)* Yes, first off, the one you call Puss-puss.

ARMANDINE: *(Quickly, jumping away from the table)* Puss-puss came here? *(She sits in the armchair to hear better.)*

GÉRÔME: Yes, she positively had to see you.

RÉDILLON: What did you tell her?

GÉRÔME: That you were with your mother! Then, since she insisted on waiting for you, I told her that when you were with your mother, you generally took three or four hours!

ARMANDINE: *(Rising)* You did the right thing! No thank you, if the two of us wound up face to face…

GÉRÔME: And then Monsieur Camembert called!

ARMANDINE: *(Back to the audience, leaning on the table)* Camembert! Wait a minute, "Camembert, Camembert"…

RÉDILLON: No, you don't know him, he's too old!

ARMANDINE: Ah! *(She turns around.)*

RÉDILLON: He's an antique dealer whose shop is on the same landing as my apartment, so occasionally, when he has a bargain...as a neighbor...

ARMANDINE: Yes, yes, you're right, it's Stilton I was thinking of, an Englishman, Stilton...I knew I'd had dealings with a cheese. *(She crosses between the table and the fireplace.)*

RÉDILLON: Yes, but it's not the same thing! *(To* GÉRÔME*)* And what did Monsieur Stilton... uh, Monsieur Camembert...want? *(To* ARMANDINE*)* You're getting me mixed up, you and your cheeses.

GÉRÔME: He told me to tell you that he had a new acquisition to show you, a rare item, a chastity belt from the fourteenth.

RÉDILLON: Ah!

ARMANDINE: *(Leaning on the table)* From the fourteenth what?

GÉRÔME: How do I know? The fourteenth cuckold, probably.

RÉDILLON: No, no, "century"! Anyone else?

GÉRÔME: No one else.

(Doorbell rings.)

GÉRÔME: Sit still, I'll get it!

RÉDILLON: I had no intention of going to the door! ...If it's a lady, I'm not in!

GÉRÔME: Y' don't have to tell me! *(He goes upstage and exits out the back.)*

ARMANDINE: *(Coming downstage)* I'll say we're not in! If that turns out to be Puss-puss again, we're in for a blow-up! Not for baby! I can't stand cat-fights! *(She goes upstage.)*

RÉDILLON: Well, where are you off to?

ARMANDINE: *(At the door at right)* Going to get dressed! If it turns out to be a woman! Then good-night, I'll blow this joint.

GÉRÔME: *(Off)* No, Madame, he isn't in! I'm sure of it! *(Sticking his head in the door at back, in a low voice to be heard only by* RÉDILLON.*)* It *is* a lady all right. Skedaddle!

RÉDILLON: Away we go! *(He exits up right.)*

GÉRÔME: *(Releasing the door at back)* Well, Madame, see for yourself, if you won't believe me!

LUCIENNE: *(Entering)* Empty!

GÉRÔME: I repeat: he isn't here!

LUCIENNE: Very well! Tell him that Madame Vatelin wants to talk to him.

GÉRÔME: Madame Vatelin! The wife of his friend Monsieur Vatelin, whom he visits so often?

LUCIENNE: Exactly.

GÉRÔME: Oh, well, that's something else again! I beg your pardon, Madame, I took you for a floozie!

LUCIENNE: Eh?

GÉRÔME: *(Calling through the door at right)* Ernest! It's Madame Vatelin!

RÉDILLON: *(Off)* What did you say?

GÉRÔME: It's Madame Vatelin! *(To* LUCIENNE*)* Here he comes!

RÉDILLON: *(Entering rapidly)* It can't be! You! You in my house… How come?… *(He motions to her to sit down.)*

LUCIENNE: *(Sitting beside the table)* Are you surprised? Ah! So am I, for that matter!

RÉDILLON: *(Undertone to* GÉRÔME*)* Tell the person in the other room to pardon me for not rejoining her, but an important matter has come up... whatever you like, and as soon as she's dressed, show her out!

GÉRÔME: Gotcha! *(He knocks on the door at right.)*

ARMANDINE; *(Off)* Don't come in!

GÉRÔME: All right! *(He goes in.)*

RÉDILLON: You! You here!

LUCIENNE: In person! You must be aware of the reason?

RÉDILLON: No!

LUCIENNE: What! If I'm here, that must mean...

RÉDILLON: What?

LUCIENNE: *(Rising and moving left)* Last night I caught my husband in the very act of adultery!

RÉDILLON: No! ...Good Lord! And you came here to make love to me!...

LUCIENNE: I never go back on my word!

(RÉDILLON, taking LUCIENNE's hands and seating her on the divan:)

RÉDILLON: Ah, Lucienne! How happy I am! Make use of me! Take me! I'm yours! *(He sits beside her.)*

LUCIENNE: No, excuse me! *I* was supposed to say that to *you*!

RÉDILLON: That's what I meant.

GÉRÔME: *(At the back)* Psst!

RÉDILLON: What?

(GÉRÔME signals him to move aside so that ARMANDINE can get by; then he closes the door at back.)

RÉDILLON: Fine!

LUCIENNE: What is it?

RÉDILLON: *(Rising)* Somebody has to come through! Here, hide behind me, there's no point in their seeing you!

(LUCIENNE rises and hides behind the back of RÉDILLON, who stands watching the upstage area. GÉRÔME passes by, accompanying the now clothed ARMANDINE. She nods a greeting to RÉDILLON, who nods back, and disappears.)

LUCIENNE: Well?

RÉDILLON: Sssh! Wait!

(GÉRÔME reappears, opens the door at back and dusts off his hands, to indicate ARMANDINE's departure.)

RÉDILLON: Yes?

(GÉRÔME nods "Yes" with a malicious little smile and withdraws.)

RÉDILLON: *(To LUCIENNE)* All right, they've gone!

LUCIENNE: Ah!

(LUCIENNE and RÉDILLON quit their positions.)

RÉDILLON: Please have a seat! *(He goes to close the door at back.)*

LUCIENNE: *(Sitting)* Would you believe such a wretch!

RÉDILLON: Who?

LUCIENNE: What who? Why, my husband, of course!

RÉDILLON: *(Sitting beside her)* Ah, yes, yes! How silly of me! I'd lost track.

LUCIENNE: And to think what a faithful wife I've been, how I've repelled the advances of poor dear Rédillon!

RÉDILLON: Yes, poor dear Rédillon!

LUCIENNE: Well, now I've stopped repelling his advances! …He loves me! …Very well! I'll be his, that's my revenge.

RÉDILLON: Yes! Ah, Lucienne, Lucienne!

GÉRÔME: *(Poking his head in at the back)* Listen! I'm going downstairs to buy a couple of lamb chops!

RÉDILLON: *(Savagely)* Go on, go on! ...We have to hear about his lamb chops... Ah, Lucienne! *(Suddenly, running to the back)* And string beans! Hey! ...String beans!...

GÉRÔME: *(Off)* All right!

RÉDILLON: *(Coming downstage)* He's got a mania for serving me potatoes every day, I'm beginning to get fed up with them! *(Sitting)* Excuse me, he's an old family retainer, a little down-to-earth. He doesn't swim in the ideal, as we do!

LUCIENNE: *(Rising and crossing left)* If you think I'm swimming in the ideal at the moment! *(She goes upstage between the table and the fireplace.)*

RÉDILLON: What was I saying just now?

LUCIENNE: You were saying he has a mania for feeding you potatoes!

RÉDILLON: *(Rising)* No, before that!

LUCIENNE: You were saying, Lucienne, Lucienne!

RÉDILLON: *(Lyrically, while trying to remember what he'd intended to say)* Ah, Lucienne, Lucienne! ...Oh yes!... *(Proceeding)* Ah, Lucienne, Lucienne!...

(RÉDILLON, *leading* LUCIENNE *back to the divan:)*

RÉDILLON: Tell me I am not the plaything of a dream! Are you really mine? No one's but mine?

LUCIENNE: *(Seated)* Yes, really and truly yours! No one's but yours!

RÉDILLON: Ah, how happy I am!

LUCIENNE: Good for you, my dear. It balances things out when some people's misfortunes make other people happy.

RÉDILLON: Yes, yes! Rest your head on my chest…

LUCIENNE: Wait, my hat's in the way. *(She takes it off.)*

RÉDILLON: Give it to me! *(He hangs it on his right fist, while his left arm encircles* LUCIENNE's *waist.)* I want to get drunk on the scent of your hair… Ah, so that's how you smell close up… and all mine!… *(He closes his eyes in ecstasy.)*

LUCIENNE: Are you going to keep holding my hat like that?

RÉDILLON: *(Rising)* No, wait.

*(*RÉDILLON *places it on the table and returns to* LUCIENNE, *who has changed her seat. Kissing her:)*

RÉDILLON: Ah, this is the first time I've been allowed to graze your skin with my lips!

LUCIENNE: That's the way! …Revenge! Revenge!

RÉDILLON: Yes!

LUCIENNE: From this day forward, I am no longer Monsieur Vatelin's wife, I am your wife… and you shall marry me!

RÉDILLON: Yes, yes!

LUCIENNE: *(Talking towards the back)* A man I loved, a man to whom I gave my all… my devotion, my fidelity… my virginal innocence.

RÉDILLON: No, no! Listen here! Stop talking about your husband…especially at this moment. Erase his image from our presence! Ah, my beloved Lucienne!… *(He kneels facing her.)*

GÉRÔME: *(Poking his head in at back)* I'm back!

RÉDILLON: Don't come in!

GÉRÔME: Hey, what are you doing in there?

RÉDILLON: Do I have to make you a report? Get out of here!…

GÉRÔME: All right!

RÉDILLON: And shut the door!

GÉRÔME: Why? Are you cold?

RÉDILLON: Because I told you to… And don't come in again until you're called.

GÉRÔME: *(Sighs and goes upstage, then, about to exit)* I couldn't find any string beans!

RÉDILLON: I couldn't care less!

GÉRÔME: So I got potatoes instead! *(He exits, closing the door.)*

RÉDILLON: I'm sorry, he's an old family retainer, but he does take advantage. Now, where were we?… *(Still on his knees)* Ah, Lucienne! Let me clasp you in my arms!

LUCIENNE: Do *you* love me?

RÉDILLON: Do I love you? …No, wait, I'm not comfortable in this position…I'm not close enough to you! Clear a little space beside you! *(He sits at her right.)*…Ah, this I way I can more easily press you to my heart!

LUCIENNE: So the gypsy fortune-teller's prediction came true!

RÉDILLON: *(Eyes half-closed)* What prediction?

LUCIENNE: That I would have two romantic adventures in my lifetime, one when I was twenty-five…the other when I'm fifty-eight. Well! the first one came true, I turned twenty-five last week.

RÉDILLON: Yes, and I'm the hero of the adventure!… *(Changing his tone)* Wait… no, this is better! *(He stretches out at full length at LUCIENNE's back, his head towards the audience.)*

LUCIENNE: What are you doing?

RÉDILLON: There! That's much better! I can see you better! ...I can possess you better!... *(He kisses her.)* Ah, Lucienne, Lucienne!

(LUCIENNE sits back in her seat.)

LUCIENNE: *(Sighing)* Ah!

(RÉDILLON's face expresses intense anxiety. He mechanically caresses LUCIENNE's hand, but it is obvious that his mind is elsewhere. She turns around to stare at him. He smiles immediately.)

LUCIENNE: Well?

RÉDILLON: What?

LUCIENNE: Is that all?

RÉDILLON: What do you mean, is that all? Ah, Lucienne, Lucienne! *(Aside)* What a rotten idea it was to bring Armandine here last night!

(LUCIENNE stares at RÉDILLON again.)

RÉDILLON: Ah, Lucienne, Lucienne!

LUCIENNE: *(Rising)* Well, what? Lucienne, Lucienne! Is that all you can say?

RÉDILLON: *(Sitting back)* Lucienne! I don't know if it's the surprise... the emotion! ...I swear this is the first time this has ever happened to me.

LUCIENNE: Oh, and this from the man who can't stop talking about his love for me!

RÉDILLON: *(Rising)* Of course I love you. Only please understand, I was so far from expecting you... So the happiness! ...The joy! ...An excess of joy! ...That's the cause. Not to mention scruples, any decent man's scruples...they won't last very long, but they *are* a justification...I can't help thinking of your husband, my friend. To play a dirty trick on him like this! …Let me have time to get used to the idea…

LUCIENNE: *(Going up to the fireplace)* Your scruples seem to be a delayed reaction, my dear!

RÉDILLON: No, they'll pass, I tell you… Just give me time to consider… Come back tomorrow! …Come back tonight!

LUCIENNE: *(Above the table)* Tomorrow! Tonight! …but that's out of the question! My husband may be here at any moment!

RÉDILLON: Huh?

LUCIENNE: *(Coming downstage)* And I hope that by the time he gets here, my revenge will be consummated.

RÉDILLON: Your husband! …Your husband here?

LUCIENNE: Yes! I dropped him a line: "You cheated on me, I'll cheat on you in return. If you doubt it, come to your friend Rédillon's at noon. *(Slightly turns her head to look at* RÉDILLON.*)* You shall find me in the arms of my lover."

RÉDILLON: But this is madness! …We were about to commit a major blunder!…That's funny, I had an intuition… Thank Heaven! Heaven has given me the strength to act rationally.

GÉRÔME: *(Off. Opposing an entrance)* No, Madame, no, no!

CLOTILDE: *(Off)* Yes, I tell you, yes!

RÉDILLON: What's this all about?

CLOTILDE: *(Pushing* GÉRÔME *away)* Leave me alone!… *(She enters.)*

RÉDILLON & LUCIENNE: Madame Pontagnac!

CLOTILDE: Precisely! In the flesh! …Ah, you didn't expect to see me here so soon, did you? …Yesterday,

Monsieur Rédillon, I told you: "Just let me get proof of my husband's infidelity and I shall come to you and say, 'Avenge me, I'm yours!'"…

LUCIENNE: Huh?

CLOTILDE: *(Taking off her jacket and throwing it on the divan)* All right, Monsieur Rédillon! Here I am! Avenge me, I'm yours!

RÉDILLON: Another one!

LUCIENNE: What's this?

RÉDILLON: *(Aside)* This is so frustrating! Good Lord! So frustrating! Oh no! *(He goes upstage to the back.)*

LUCIENNE: Excuse me, Madame. "Avenge me, I'm yours…" Your behavior is rather bold.

CLOTILDE: How's that, Madame! It was an agreement made with Monsieur Rédillon.

LUCIENNE: But excuse me, Madame. I was here ahead of you!

CLOTILDE: That may very well be, Madame, but allow me to observe that I reserved Monsieur Rédillon since yesterday.

LUCIENNE: You reserved him? Ah, very well, that makes no difference to me!

CLOTILDE: Madame!

LUCIENNE: Madame!

RÉDILLON: *(Intervening between them)* For heaven's sake, don't I have anything to say in the matter?

LUCIENNE: True enough! You choose!

CLOTILDE: By all means! You choose!

RÉDILLON: Very well, I shall choose. This is amazing. Honestly! You want to take revenge on your respective husbands… so I'm supposed to… Do you accept me as the official agent of conjugal retribution?

LUCIENNE: Hurry up, which one of us?

CLOTILDE: Yes?

RÉDILLON: Well, neither one! There!

CLOTILDE & LUCIENNE: Huh?

RÉDILLON: Good night!… *(He crosses center.)*

CLOTILDE & LUCIENNE: Oh!

GÉRÔME: *(Running in at the back)* Listen… it's Puss-puss!

RÉDILLON: What! Puss-puss!

GÉRÔME: She's back again! She wants to see you!

RÉDILLON: Puss-puss as well! Oh no! I've had enough, once and for all! I won't see her! Tell her I died!

GÉRÔME: Very good! *(He exits.)*

CLOTILDE & LUCIENNE: *(Together)* Rédillon! —Monsieur Rédillon!

RÉDILLON: No! *(He exits right and locks himself in.)*

CLOTILDE & LUCIENNE: *(Rush simultaneously to the door)* Locked!

CLOTILDE: *(Coming down left)* You see, Madame, it's all your fault.

LUCIENNE: Excuse me, Madame, it's yours!

CLOTILDE: *(With a caustic laugh)* It's mine! If you only understood, Madame, how distressing this course of action is for me!

LUCIENNE: But, Madame, do you think *I'm* here for fun?

CLOTILDE: No thank you! If I weren't driven to it by the need for revenge.

LUCIENNE: Me too!

CLOTILDE: Is that all you can say— Me too!

LUCIENNE: What am I supposed to say, since our situations are identical!

CLOTILDE: And these are the shifts our husbands reduce us to!

LUCIENNE: It's hard on a respectable woman!

GÉRÔME: *(Appearing at the back)* Madame, there's a young man asking for Madame Vatelin.

LUCIENNE: Asking for me! …A young man! …Who's that?

GÉRÔME: Monsieur Pontagnac!

CLOTILDE: *(Who has gone upstage to the fireplace)* My husband!

LUCIENNE: Is that what you call a young man?

GÉRÔME: He's young compared to me! …Remember, Madame, I had already come of age when he was still at the nipple.

CLOTILDE: But what does my husband want?

LUCIENNE: I don't know! He's asking for me… As a matter of fact! He's just in time! I need an avenger!

CLOTILDE: What, you're going to…?

LUCIENNE: Oh, don't worry! It's only to put my husband off the scent.

CLOTILDE: Oh, in that case!

LUCIENNE: Will you lend me Monsieur Pontagnac?

CLOTILDE: All right. Besides, it'll give me one more grievance against him!

LUCIENNE: Fine! *(Takes CLOTILDE's jacket and hands it to her.)* Here, Madame, step in there!

(LUCIENNE shows CLOTILDE out up left. To GÉRÔME:)

LUCIENNE: And you, show in Monsieur Pontagnac!

GÉRÔME: Yes, Madame. *(Aside)* I'm not following any of this!

(GÉRÔME shows in PONTAGNAC and vanishes.)

PONTAGNAC: *(Entering, highly emotional)* Alone at last!

LUCIENNE: Were you asking for me?

PONTAGNAC: Here I am! Have you been here long?

LUCIENNE: I just got here!

PONTAGNAC: What about...Rédillon?

LUCIENNE: I'm waiting for him!

PONTAGNAC: Saints be praised, I'm in time. *(He puts his hat on the table.)*

LUCIENNE: But what's the big idea of coming and forcing yourself on me here? What do you want?

PONTAGNAC: What do I want? I want to stop you from committing a folly! ...I want to step between you and Rédillon, to plead with you, to snatch you from him!

LUCIENNE: You! And what right have you?

PONTAGNAC: What right? ...Why, the right given me by all the nuisances I've had to put up with since yesterday! ...Out of love for you, I got involved in the most ghastly scrapes. I've been blamed for two acts of adultery! ...Adulteries I never even knew about! ...Nabbed by a husband I don't know from Adam... on account of a wife I don't know from Eve! Nabbed by my own wife, on account of the wife I don't know! ...A possible divorce in my future! ...Another divorce by the lady I don't know from the gentleman I don't know in which I am going to be cited as co-respondent! ...In the doghouse with Madame Pontagnac! The wife I don't know came round this morning to tell

me in a German accent that I owe her "respiration"!
An altercation, complicated by assault and battery,
with the gentleman I don't know! In short, headaches,
lawsuits, scandal, the lot! And all this just to fling you
into the arms of another man! ...He'll win the jackpot
and I have to be the loser! ...Oh, no, no! You wouldn't
want that!

LUCIENNE: *(Aside)* Just you wait!... *(Aloud)* Goodness!
...what a coincidence! ...Imagine, when I saw you
show up just now I said to myself, "Well, why Rédillon
anyway? After all, it was Monsieur Pontagnac who
informed me of my husband's infidelity!"

PONTAGNAC: Definitely!

LUCIENNE: If anyone is to avenge me, it ought to be
him!

PONTAGNAC: No! I can't believe it...

LUCIENNE: So, if I were to ask you...

PONTAGNAC: If you were to ask me! ...You know I'd be
the happiest of men!...

LUCIENNE: Really? Well, be the happiest of men! You,
Monsieur Pontagnac, shall be my avenger!

PONTAGNAC: No?

LUCIENNE: Yes!

PONTAGNAC: Can it be! And here at Pinkillon's... uh,
Rédillon's! What a delicious twist! *(He goes to close the
door at back and lower the blinds.)*

LUCIENNE: *(Going to the table)* Come on then! *(She
removes the garment which covers her under-bodice and
appears in a very low-cut black velvet, sleeveless evening-
gown with diamanté shoulder-straps, while she unfastens
her hair with a toss of the head.)* This was the way my
husband used to think me at my loveliest! Am I really
beautiful like this?

PONTAGNAC: *(Removing his gloves)* Oh yes! beautiful! As beautiful as the sinful Princess of Baghdad in the new novel!

LUCIENNE: Obviously. I was just rereading it this morning.

PONTAGNAC: What for?

LUCIENNE: Because! ...Because I'm not accustomed to this sort of vengeance. I wanted to pick up the right tone! *(Changing to a melodramatic tone)* And do you love me?

PONTAGNAC: *(Holding her in his arms)* Profoundly!

LUCIENNE: *(Aside)* Well, it looks as if he knows his lines! *(Aloud)* And your whole life will be mine?

PONTAGNAC: My whole life.

LUCIENNE: *(Leaving him and crossing left)* All right, sit down!

PONTAGNAC: *(Astonished)* What do you mean, sit down?

LUCIENNE: Do it!

PONTAGNAC: But I thought...

LUCIENNE: Did I deny it? ...But I don't feel like it at the moment. Suppose I decide to choose my moment, to make myself desirable. I expect any man who loves me will be the obedient slave of my whims. I said, "Sit down"! Sit down!

(PONTAGNAC sits next to the table.)

LUCIENNE: *(Going a bit upstage)* Good!

PONTAGNAC: I obeyed you!

LUCIENNE: *(Coming to him)* Very good! Take off your jacket.

PONTAGNAC: Beg pardon!

LUCIENNE: *(Moving right)* Take off your jacket! I can't bear to see you with it on. You remind me of my husband.

PONTAGNAC: Ah! in that case. However, I warn you that I'll be in shirt-sleeves underneath.

LUCIENNE: *(Sitting on the divan)* That doesn't matter.

PONTAGNAC: Fine. *(He takes off his jacket.)* Now what?

LUCIENNE: Sit next to me.

PONTAGNAC: *(Sitting)* All right.

LUCIENNE: Good.

(A moment of silence.)

PONTAGNAC: *(After a pause)* Well, what are we waiting for?

LUCIENNE: When I'm good and ready!

PONTAGNAC: Ah!

LUCIENNE: Here, take off your vest. You look like a moving-man this way.

PONTAGNAC: What? You want...

LUCIENNE: Please, and then sit down again.

PONTAGNAC: *(Takes off his vest and puts it down at the back)* This is only because you command it. *(Sitting)* Don't you think I look absurd this way?

LUCIENNE: Don't give it another thought! *(Unbuttoning one of his suspenders.)* That's so ugly! ...Like those draft horses! ...And who does your hair like that? ...A head waiter's hair style.

PONTAGNAC: *(Who has unbuttoned the other suspender)* Oh!

LUCIENNE: Turn around! *(Mussing up his back hair.)* There! Now at least you look like an artist.

PONTAGNAC: Think so? *(Forgetting his promises)* Ah, Lucienne, my Lucienne!

LUCIENNE: Hey! What's all this?

PONTAGNAC: Oh! Sorry!

LUCIENNE: Please control yourself, won't you, when there's nobody around.

PONTAGNAC: Whatever you say, but I'm only flesh and blood!

LUCIENNE: That's all I require!

PONTAGNAC: Fine!

(LUCIENNE has risen and gone to take a newspaper from the table, then comes back, sits down and starts leafing through it.)

PONTAGNAC: *(Having watched her; after a pause)* What an odd way to make love. *(Reading the headline)* "The Daily Republican."

LUCIENNE: *(After a pause)* Ah! There's a play opening at the Déjazet tonight.

PONTAGNAC: Aha!

LUCIENNE: You going?

PONTAGNAC: No!

LUCIENNE: Ah!…

(LUCIENNE goes on reading. PONTAGNAC, not knowing what to do, starts whistling and looking around. Finally, he gets up and, hands behind his back, inspects the knick-knacks.)

LUCIENNE: *(Not lifting her head from the paper)* Stay put!

PONTAGNAC: Ah! Fine! *(He sits down again docilely; after a pause.)* After all, what am I waiting for? …Forced to be polite so I'll get a piece of candy!

(A sound of voices at the back)

LUCIENNE: Sssh!

PONTAGNAC: *(Who has risen at the sound)* What is it?

*(*LUCIENNE *has arisen at the same time and crumples up the newspaper, throwing it away.)*

LUCIENNE: *(Aside)* At last!… *(Aloud)* What do we care! People! …My husband, perhaps.

PONTAGNAC: Your husband!

LUCIENNE: Better and better! My revenge will be all the sweeter.

(At that moment the blinds at the back fly up and heads appear at the windows.)

INSPECTOR: *(Off)* Open up in the name of the law!

PONTAGNAC: It's them! Hide!

LUCIENNE: Hide indeed! Do you love me enough to fight my husband for me?

PONTAGNAC: Of course, but…

INSPECTOR: *(Off)* Are you going to open up?

LUCIENNE: Very well! I wish to be yours before the eyes of the world! Pontagnac, take me, I'm yours.

PONTAGNAC: What? Now?

LUCIENNE: Now or never!

PONTAGNAC: *(Pulling away)* Oh no, really!

INSPECTOR: Open up or I'll break the glass.

LUCIENNE: Go ahead, open up or he'll break the glass.

PONTAGNAC: *(Aghast)* Huh? Right!

*(*PONTAGNAC *opens the door.* LUCIENNE *drops seated on to the divan, stretches out her legs, crossing them, her body flung back, resting on her arms. She casts her husband a look of defiance.)*

VATELIN: *(Entering)* Oh, the shameless hussy!…

INSPECTOR: Don't nobody move!

VATELIN: It was true!

PONTAGNAC: *(To the* INSPECTOR*)* See here, Monsieur.

INSPECTOR: *(Glaring at him)* You again, Monsieur! This is rather frequent!

PONTAGNAC: But, Monsieur, I don't understand. I was paying a call on this lady.

INSPECTOR: In that state of undress! Put your clothes on, Monsieur.

*(*PONTAGNAC *gets dressed, forgetting to adjust his suspenders.)*

RÉDILLON: *(Coming out of his room down right; facing the audience)* Well, what's going on in here?

INSPECTOR: Madame, I am the police inspector for your district, and I'm here at the request of Monsieur Crispin Vatelin, your husband…

RÉDILLON: Allow me to interrupt. An attempted adultery in my house? *(Aside)* Pontagnac?

LUCIENNE: *(In the same posture as before)* That's all right, Inspector, I know the speech. *(Aside)* I read it in the novel this morning! *(Aloud)* So I'm going to save you some trouble. Monsieur Pontagnac may tell you whatever he wishes to try and exonerate me, that's his duty as a gentleman, but I intend the truth to be known to all.

*(*LUCIENNE, *defiantly glaring at* VATELIN *who stands between the table and the fireplace, almost with his back to his wife:)*

LUCIENNE: Nothing seduced me here except my own free will and my pleasure, and if I left home it was to find my lover, Monsieur Pontagnac!

VATELIN: She confesses.

LUCIENNE: Inspector, I authorize you to include this confession in the report.

VATELIN: *(Dropping on to the chair near the fireplace)* Oh!

CLOTILDE: *(Appearing at the door at left)* Now it's my turn!

PONTAGNAC: My wife!

CLOTILDE: Please include as well, Inspector, that you found me, Clotilde Pontagnac, this gentleman's legitimate spouse, in this house, where I had come, like this lady, to meet my lover.

PONTAGNAC: *(Surging forward)* What did she say?

CLOTILDE: Good-bye, Monsieur. *(She exits left.)*

PONTAGNAC: *(Running after her, his suspenders flapping against his thighs)* Hussy!

INSPECTOR: *(Stopping him)* Please remain, Monsieur. You are required to.

PONTAGNAC: But you heard what she said, Inspector, she has a lover.

(The INSPECTOR shrugs, coming downstage.)

PONTAGNAC: Where is the wretch, let me strangle him, let me kill him!

GÉRÔME: *(Aside)* He wants to hurt my Ernest, my baby boy!

PONTAGNAC: *(Walking around furiously)* Just let this lover show himself if he's not a coward!

GÉRÔME: *(Stepping forward)* It's me!

PONTAGNAC: You!

RÉDILLON: *(To GÉRÔME)* What are you saying?

GÉRÔME: *(Undertone to RÉDILLON)* Shut up. I'm saving your life!

PONTAGNAC: Very good, Monsieur, we shall meet again! Your card!

GÉRÔME: I haven't got one! ...But I'm Gérôme, Ernest's valet... my little Ernest's valet... *(He pats* RÉDILLON's *cheek and goes upstage.)*

PONTAGNAC: A valet!

INSPECTOR: *(Coming downstage to* PONTAGNAC*)* Can't you see they're pulling your leg. So is Madame Pontagnac! ...Don't you understand that it was the fib of an outraged wife and not the confession of a guilty spouse?

PONTAGNAC: *(Going upstage between the table and the fireplace and taking his hat)* Oh, I'll find out!

INSPECTOR: *(Going upstage)* In the meantime, we require your presence. Is there something to write with?

RÉDILLON: In there, Inspector. *(He indicates the room at back.)*

INSPECTOR: Thank you, Monsieur. *(To* PONTAGNAC.*)* Will you please step this way, Monsieur and... Madame...

LUCIENNE: All right! *(She rises and goes slowly upstage, still fixedly watching her husband. Halfway there, restraining her emotion with difficulty, her face contracts with sobs and, pointing to her husbands, says, without a sound, merely moving her lips:)* A man to whom I gave all my love!

(At that moment, VATELIN, *to save face, rises and scornfully turns his head towards his wife.* LUCIENNE *instantly recovers her expression of bravado.)*

LUCIENNE: *(Flinging her head back)* Let's go!

(She enters the room at back, where everyone, except RÉDILLON *and* VATELIN, *has gone. In that room, the* INSPECTOR'S *secretary, one of the two policemen, is seated*

at a table. The INSPECTOR *stands near him, dictating the report.* GÉRÔME *has disappeared.* LUCIENNE *and* PONTAGNAC *are standing one on either side of the table.)*

(VATELIN, *at his wits' end, has fallen into an armchair, face in hands, sobbing heartbroken. He has placed his hat on the table.)*

RÉDILLON: Well, here's a nice mess! *(Seeing* VATELIN*)* Come, come, Vatelin!

VATELIN: Ah, my friend, you've no idea the agonizing torment! In here...going boom, boom, boom! *(He indicates his temples.)*

RÉDILLON: *(Clapping him on the shoulder)* There, there! It doesn't matter! It doesn't matter!

VATELIN: It doesn't matter...to you! But to me... Good grief! If it concerned some other man's wife, it wouldn't matter to me either, but to think that my own wedded wife is one who cheats on me! ...That's too hard!

RÉDILLON: Will you allow me to speak frankly as a friend?

VATELIN: Please do, my friend!

RÉDILLON: Well, Vatelin, my friend, you are a nitwit!

VATELIN: You think so?

RÉDILLON: Absolutely!

VATELIN: A cuckolded nitwit, in that case!

RÉDILLON: No, not cuckolded! Thinking that way is what makes you a nitwit. Look here! Isn't her note to you, "Come to Rédillon's flat. You'll find me in the arms of my lover" enough to set you straight? ... A woman two-timing her husband doesn't usually send him an invitation.

VATELIN: True enough! ...But then?...

RÉDILLON: Well, if she did it, she must have had a reason! She wanted to provoke her husband's jealousy. To quote the Inspector: Can't you see that as the farce of an outraged wife taking revenge! ...Everything suggests it, that insistence on self-accusation...

VATELIN: Yes...

RÉDILLON: That set-up...

VATELIN: Yes...

RÉDILLON: That caught-in-the-act costume...

VATELIN: Yes...

RÉDILLON: That choice of Pontagnac whom she's known only since yesterday.

VATELIN: Yes...

RÉDILLON: In fact, I know something about all this. She first suggested that *I* play the part... which I turned down. *(Aside)* and a good thing too!

VATELIN: *(Holding out his hands to him)* Ah, my friend, my friend!

RÉDILLON: *(Taking his hands)* And you fell right into the trap... Ah, you aren't much of a clear thinker!

VATELIN: I'm an attorney.

RÉDILLON: There you have it!

VATELIN: Ah, I'm so glad!... *(Sobbing.)* I'm so hap... hap... py! Oh dear, dear! Oh, dear, dear! *(He weeps into his hands.)*

RÉDILLON: This happiness is most alarming!

(At that moment, the door at back opens and LUCIENNE *comes downstage with the same arrogant expression; she stops in astonishment and stares questioningly at* RÉDILLON, *who, putting a finger to his lips, signals her to be silent and listen.)*

VATELIN: I'm so happy!…

RÉDILLON: Come, come, moderate your rapture!

VATELIN: Ah, my friend, be kind! Find my wife and tell her I've never loved anyone but her, and make her understand—this is the truth—that I've been the most faithful of husbands.

RÉDILLON: After your escapade of last night?

VATELIN: Well, if you think last night's escapade was fun! I wish you could have been there, at last night's escapade!

RÉDILLON: I should have thought myself a third wheel!

VATELIN: You should have been there, anyway! Oh dear oh dear oh dear! That Viennese woman…with feet like gunboats. No, I should have brought you one of her shoes…I never, except for that episode in Vienna—I know it's idiotic to confess this—I never cheated on my wife, except once in Vienna. I had to, away for a month, no wife—a man's not made of wood—. At least I thought it was all over and done with. Ah! well, she showed up yesterday at my house. Talk about a public nuisance, she was a private nuisance. She threatened to make a scene, I was afraid to destroy my wife's happiness and so I gave in.

RÉDILLON: Ah, what a shame your wife can't hear this.

(RÉDILLON *looks at* LUCIENNE *who begins to weaken.*)

VATELIN: Yes, it is a shame she can't hear this. I'm sure I could convince her, that she'd believe me. I'd become so contrite, so repentant. She'd see so much love in my eyes that she couldn't have the heart to reject me. I'd hold out my hand to her, she'd clasp it with her little hand, and I'd hear her beloved voice say, "Crispin dear, I forgive you!"

(RÉDILLON *has taken* LUCIENNE'*s hand and slips it into* VATELIN'*s.*)

LUCIENNE: Crispin, I forgive you!...

VATELIN: *(Rising)* You! Ah, you wicked girl, how you hurt me! *(He falls sobbing into her arms.)*

LUCIENNE: And what about *you*?

VATELIN: I adore you!

LUCIENNE: Darling!

RÉDILLON: *(Turns his back to hide his emotion; unable to resist, tears in his voice)* I love both of you!

VATELIN: *(Shaking his hand, as does* LUCIENNE*)* Dear friend!...

(All three kiss.)

VATELIN: *(To* LUCIENNE*)* Ah, he's been very good!

*(*RÉDILLON *and* LUCIENNE *cross to center.)*

INSPECTOR: *(Entering and coming downstage)* The report is drawn up, if you wish to read it over.

VATELIN: The report! We don't need any more reports! There's no more reason for any reports! *(Crossing to* LUCIENNE.*)* We'll tear up all the reports!...

INSPECTOR: Huh?

VATELIN: Go ahead, Inspector, tear up the report!... *(He pulls him to the back.)*

INSPECTOR: How did I get mixed up with this set of flibbertigibbets!

RÉDILLON: *(Alone on stage with* LUCIENNE*)* Well?

LUCIENNE: Well?

RÉDILLON: Back where we started!

LUCIENNE: Back where we started!

RÉDILLON: *(Smiling)* And what about me, have I had it?

LUCIENNE: You've had it… and yet! You know the fortune-teller told me I was to have two adventures in my lifetime. The first one is over and done with, the second one when I'm fifty-eight. Are you tempted?

RÉDILLON: Hmm! Fifty-eight!

LUCIENNE: Well, really!

RÉDILLON: Oh, not on your account, you'll still be charming, but I'll be very worn out.

LUCIENNE: *(Mildly sarcastic)* As usual!

(VATELIN comes downstage followed by PONTAGNAC.)

VATELIN: Now it's all been settled! As for you, Pontagnac, I ought to hold it against you, but no hard feelings! And to prove it, I invite you to dinner every Monday. Will you be one of our regulars?

PONTAGNAC: Me! What?… Why, of course!

VATELIN: Just a stag dinner! That's the night my wife dines with her mother!

PONTAGNAC: *(Getting the moral)* Ah, with pleasure! *(Aside)* There's nothing cooking anymore!

RÉDILLON: *(Undertone to LUCIENNE)* All the same, if the fancy takes you again some time, well! warn me the night before!

GÉRÔME: *(At the back)* When are you coming to lunch?

RÉDILLON: Right now!

(VATELIN, LUCIENNE, RÉDILLON go a bit upstage.)

PONTAGNAC: *(Coming downstage, aside)* It was in the cards: I'm the loser! *(He joins them.)*

(Curtain)

END OF PLAY

www.ingramcontent.com/pod-product-compliance
Lightning Source LLC
Chambersburg PA
CBHW052105090426
42741CB00009B/1690